21 YEARS OF
JACK THE RIPPER AND
THE WHITECHAPEL
SOCIETY

First edition published 2016
Softcover edition 2019

Copyright © The Whitechapel Society, 2016/2019

The right of The Whitechapel Society to be identified as the author of this work has been asserted in accordance with the Copyright, Designs & Patents Act 1988.

Publisher's note: Although the articles contained in this book remain as originally written, certain formatting has been edited to ensure consistency across the book.

All rights reserved. No part of this book may be reprinted or reproduced or utilised in any form or by any electronic, mechanical or other means, now known or hereafter invented, including photocopying and recording, or in any information storage or retrieval system, without the prior permission in writing of the publishers.

ISBN: 978-1-911273-54-7 (softcover)
ISBN: 978-1-911273-08-0 (ebook)

Published by Mango Books
www.MangoBooks.co.uk
18 Soho Square
London W1D 3QL

21 YEARS OF JACK THE RIPPER AND THE WHITECHAPEL SOCIETY

CONTENTS

Introduction i

1995: The Miller's Court Mystery 1

1996: Streets of Whitechapel... 6

1997: "Pictures, Paint, and Prosceniums".. 26

1998: "The Foulest Deed of Modern Times" 32

1999: Mary Kelly: The (Not So) Simple Truth 40

2000: The Lusk Kidney Revisited.. 47

2001: Robert James Lees: The Myth and the Man 61

2002: Mary Kelly is Dead... 79

2003: My Search for Jack the Ripper.. 87

2004: London Correspondence... 106

2005: The Attempted Murder at Mile End 117

2006: Sergeant William Thick.. 123

2007: Frederick Deeming: Was He Jack the Ripper?........................... 132

2008: Who Was Annie Millwood? 139

2009: A Tangled Skein? 147

2010: Thomas Oliver Weston.. 158

2011: George Hutchinson: Witness, Suspect or Red Herring................... 169

2012: Watt Do You Think The True Identity of Jack the Ripper Was? 174

2013: The Diary of Jack the Ripper: 20 Years On 184

2014: The Metropolitan Police and Working-Class Women in the Late 1880s.. 198

2015: A Letter to the Home Secretary: The State and the Ripper 207

INTRODUCTION

MARK GALLOWAY, PRESIDENT OF THE WHITECHAPEL SOCIETY

When I started the Whitechapel Society (formerly the Cloak and Dagger Club) back in 1995, never did I dream that 21 years later the Society would still be going strong and have something in the order of 300 members worldwide. The Society is unique in being the first club of its kind devoted to the study of Jack the Ripper. However, in more recent years, its remit has widened to include all aspects of the social history of the East End of London from late Victorian to early Edwardian times.

Ripperologist magazine started its life as the members' newsletter of the Cloak and Dagger Club. Initially in paper format, this has now become the world's foremost online magazine dealing with the subject of Jack the Ripper.

When the Cloak and Dagger Club became The Whitechapel Society, it produced its own magazine, *The Whitechapel Journal*. This is published six times a year and is ably edited by Frogg Moody and Samantha Hulass. As well as club news, it contains interesting, well-written and well-researched articles.

I hope you enjoy this collection of articles taken from both *Ripperologist* and latterly *The Whitechapel Journal*. My task was to select one article from each of the 21 years. This was extremely hard to do as there have been so many brilliant pieces of work. My final choice is what you will find in this book, and I am very grateful to all those authors who so willingly gave their permission for us to use their work again. But I would also like to thank all the authors, researchers and amateurs alike who have made such valuable contributions to our magazines over the years.

I would also like to thank all the committee, past and present, for everything they have done to bring the society to where it is today. I would particularly like to thank Sue Parry for all the work she has done on this book, from contacting the authors of the articles through to scanning some of the articles and converting them into Word documents. I know she has spent a lot of time on this and she would want to thank Phil Parry and Samantha Hulass for their time and patience with proofreading the many chapters.

Thanks must also go to Adam Wood of Mango Books for publishing this book and for his design work.

To find out more about The Whitechapel Society, the two-monthly meetings, the special events and *The Whitechapel Journal*, please go to our website: www.whitechapelsociety.com

1995
THE MILLER'S COURT MYSTERY

CLAUDIA OLIVER

*This article appeared in the third edition of
The Cloak & Dagger Club newsletter*

Whitechapel 1888, and London is exposed to one of its worst menaces of the late 19th century - Jack the Ripper! The man and the myth may have little on 20th century serial killers such as Jeffrey Dahmer and the Moors Murderers, but the name is burnt into criminal history forever. However, the Whitechapel murders are not as straightforward a case as many may think, regardless of the speculation surrounding the killer's identity and whether he did indeed give himself his chilling nickname. A twist to the story concerns others involved, those who have received little press. Who else knew the killer? One witness report from the time suggests that Catharine Eddowes, murdered on September 30th in Mitre Square as part of the "double event", may have known her killer and had returned from a working holiday in Kent to earn the £100 police reward offered for his capture. This is what she told the superintendent at a casual ward she visited though it was not something she ever related to her common-law husband John Kelly. As much mystery surrounds the life and death of the supposed fifth victim Mary Jane Kelly as it does the murderer. One of the newest

The entrance to Miller's Court in 1929

theories, now increasing in popularity and holding substantial credibility, is the possibility that Mary Kelly was not murdered at 13 Miller's Court in the early hours of Friday 9th November, but escaped the killer's knife. At 4.00am on that day a cry of "Oh murder!" was heard to come from the direction of number 13. It was not a cry generally associated with a young woman as her murderer drew his knife across her throat. But it would be relevant if someone had unexpectedly discovered a murder victim.

At 8.00am a Dorset Street resident Maurice Lewis saw Mary Kelly leave her room and then return a few moments later.

At 8.30am Mary was again seen, this time at the entrance to the court. Here she spoke to Caroline Maxwell, wife of a Dorset Street lodging house deputy. Mary had been sick on the roadside and complained of feeling ill. Caroline went on her way and on returning about half an hour later saw her outside the Britannia public house in Dorset Street talking to a man she thought looked like a porter.

At 10.00am Maurice again saw Mary, this time in the Horn of Plenty public house at the opposite end of Dorset Street drinking with friends.

At 10.45am the body was discovered in number 13 Miller's Court by the rent collector chasing up Mary's overdue rent payments.

These people could not have been mistaken about whom they saw. Maurice had known Mary for the past few years and Caroline knew her from being in the lodging house. Criticism from various researchers that they must have seen Mary's ghost or had the day or time wrong is simply sweeping annoying facts and doubts under the carpet.

A police surgeon arrived at Miller's Court in the afternoon and concluded that death would have occurred between one and two in the morning.

The day before the murder Mary had been seen talking to a well-dressed stranger in the court. Later she was seen by a woman talking to another stranger. This woman claimed to have been accosted in Bethnal Green not a week previously by the same man.

That evening Mary drank in the Horn of Plenty with a woman named Elizabeth Foster. She was never traced in the investigations that followed.

In the early hours of November 9th Mary was seen with a man and a woman. The man asked the other woman "Will you?" She turned away.

If, as witness reports suggest, Mary was not murdered in the early hours of that day then what happened to her? Where did she go? She had often spoken of returning to her family in Ireland. Is that where she ended up? And what happened to Jack the Ripper who also mysteriously disappeared that same day? The opinion of Whitechapel and Spitalfields locals at the time was that Mary knew the killer.

Attempts to trace the most unidentified of all the Ripper's "victims" and her family in her native Limerick and childhood home in Wales have failed to bring to light any concrete evidence as to her background.

But are researchers looking in the right place? With the alleged existence of Inspector Abberline's diaries which claim her real name was Mary Jane O'Brien, a whole new avenue of investigation is opened up. News of the final murder was published in two Limerick newspapers but provoked no response from the public. Mary Jane Kelly did not exist. But Mary Jane O'Brien did.

If she did return to her family's side, possibly with the Ripper, there would have been no reason for family and friends to suspect anything. John McCarthy, Mary's landlord, claimed that she received letters from Ireland so she was still in contact with someone there.

And what happened to the mysterious Elizabeth Foster? Was she an alias for Winifred May Collis, a friend of Mary's from her days in Cleveland Street, West London? According to Abberline's diaries she went to stay with Mary in the East End in November 1888 due to an unwanted pregnancy and was never heard of again.

The authenticity of the diaries has yet to be proved but what is almost certain is that Mary was three months pregnant in November and she was seriously considering an abortion. No trace of pregnancy was found in the body removed from 13 Miller's Court and all the organs for this to have occurred were present and correct. The only organ missing was the heart.

But what grounds can there be for the possibility that Mary knew her killer? For one she had a personal fear of being struck down by the Ripper and she contemplated suicide in the autumn of 1888. She was also seeing another man behind her common-law husband, Joseph Barnett's, back.

His name was Joe and he beat Mary sometimes for staying with Barnett though close friends thought she would marry him. Was she carrying this man's child and if so how far would he have gone to get her back - blackmail through murder?

If he found out about her abortion plans and caught her with an abortionist, whether professional or amateur, would he have removed her?

This horrific act of violence would certainly have prevented Mary from returning to her sanctuary in the court. It might explain why she was still wandering around Dorset Street half an hour before the body was discovered. She was lucky to escape and someone must have had a hand in her disappearance.

Mary was known to use a pub near Monument called the Britannia. After the murders of Elizabeth Stride and Catharine Eddowes she stopped going there. Was she trying to avoid someone as a result of which nothing happened during October? The list of evidence to prove "The Kelly Connection" is endless.

To say that the Ripper was cunning enough to escape detection is a little inaccurate to say the least. If the police of 1888 had co-operated and had taken as much notice of Whitechapel's locals as some theorists do today, Jack the Ripper might not have gone unidentified...

1996
STREETS OF WHITECHAPEL

PAUL DANIEL

This article was published in Ripperologist issue 7 (September 1996) and re-edited in 2002

The proliferation of streets carrying the same name in the Whitechapel area of the nineteenth century is quite extraordinary (though several had changed their names by 1888) - two White's Rows, two North Streets, two John Streets, two Montague Streets, three Church Streets, three Devonshire Streets, three George Streets, and others, all within a very close proximity to each other, making the area map very confusing. For instance: it is clear that Liz Stride and Michael Kidney lived in the Devonshire Street that ran southwards from Commercial Road as she had given her address in full to the Swedish Church in 1886, but in which George Street did Emma Smith live? In which George Street did Mary Kelly live in 1887 when she met Joe Barnett - and was it the same George Street in which Satchell's Lodging House was sited? The confusion is made worse when one realizes that two of the George Streets were parallel to each other, and barely three hundred yards apart. But this particular riddle is solved when one discovers that the easterly George Street changed its name to Casson Street on 12th October 1883 - before either Smith or Kelly lived in George Street (and, of course, Joe Barnett did actually state at Kelly's inquest that it was

George Street, Commercial Road at which they lived...)

In these notes, I have tried to put forward some lesser known facts! I have tried to place the streets more firmly in the mental map of the area, and include something of interest for each street mentioned. The first section is devoted to the five main sites of the Whitechapel murders - whereas the second section includes (hopefully) some interesting things about some of the less important streets connected to the case.

THE MURDER SITES

Buck's Row, the site of the murder of Mary Ann 'Polly' Nichols, now generally accepted as the first of the Ripper's victims, lay parallel to the Whitechapel Road just behind Whitechapel Underground Station (opened on 6th October 1884, a mere four years before Polly's death) and led from Brady Street (whose name had been changed from North Street on 7th May 1875) in the east, through to Baker's Row (now Vallance Road) at the west. Originally this narrow road terminated at Thomas Street (later changed to Fulbourne Street) where it became White's Row for the short distance to Baker's Row..... odd, as there was already a White's Row a mere half mile away, just south of the notorious Dorset Street, and which is still there today. The only registered business in Buck's Row was Miss Louisa Wise, who was a dressmaker at No. 26, presumably working from home. All the residential houses were on the south side of the street, the north being taken up with warehouses, which included Essex Wharf, at this time occupied by James Brown, Son and Blomfield, builders, and James Brown, brick maker (no doubt related). Walter Purkiss, the manager of the Wharf, and his wife, who lived there, heard nothing at the time of Polly Nichols murder, which was committed directly opposite the wharf by a gateway to a yard beside New Cottage (No. 2) where Mrs. Emma Green lived with her family, two sons and a daughter. The houses of both Buck's Row and Winthrop Street (previously known as Little North Street) have long since been demolished, though it is still possible to see the width of Winthrop Street (about ten feet of actual roadway) as the curbs still survive into 1996, but I fear, not for much longer as there is already a large block of post-modern dwellings, almost completed, which covers the ground between the two streets. The only building that still survives from the 1880s is the Board School at the west end of Winthrop Street, which links that street to Durward Street. It has been completely derelict for many years, but is currently surrounded by scaffolding, and is supposedly being converted into flats and a health centre, presumably to help 'gentrify' the area which has been built up during 1996. Buck's Row and White's Row were joined to become Durward Street on 25th October 1892 and Daniel Farson, in his book *Jack The Ripper* (1972) tells a nice story of why this came about: when the respectable residents became disillusioned with living in such a 'notorious' street, where the postman's macabre joke of knocking on a door and saying "Number... Killer's Row, I believe" became too much, they finally petitioned for the name to be changed - and it was! On the northern side of the west end of Buck's Row, Kearley and Tonge, of Mitre Square, had another warehouse.

29 Hanbury Street: The site of the second of the Ripper's murders, that of Annie Chapman. Hanbury Street was also, and still is, parallel to Whitechapel Road but further north and more to the west. It started just a few yards up Baker's Row from Durward Street's west end, and travelled through to terminate at Commercial Street, just a little north of Hawksmoor's Christ Church, Spitalfields. No 29 stood on the northern side of what was previously Brown's Lane, which ran from Commercial Street to Brick Lane, where it changed its name to Montague Street. It then became Preston Street and again for the rest of the distance to Baker's Row it was known as Church Street - odd, again, as the other Church Street (now renamed Fournier Street) beside Christ Church, was so close. These four streets were amalgamated into Hanbury Street on 31st March 1876. At No. 23 was the Black Swan pub which was managed by a certain Thomas David Roberts, and at no 23A, reached through a passage to the left of the pub, were Joseph and Thomas Bayley, who were case packers - maybe they used cases made by Amelia Richardson, listed in the *Post Office Street Directory* as a packing-case maker of 29

Hanbury Street... The site of these houses is now covered by a large and particularly ugly modern block owned by Truman's Brewery, and built in the early 1970s. On 14th October 1896 a certain Robert Winthrop (a strange coincidence here) was born in this street, his (very large) family living just in from Commercial Road at No. 12. His father, Wolf, was a grocer and boot-finisher... an odd combination although actually starting out in life with the name of Chaim Reuben Weintrop, Robert eventually became the much-loved comedian, singer and actor Bud Flanagan, partner of Chesney Allen and member of the famous Crazy Gang.

Berner Street: This street was situated in the Parish of St George in the East and renamed Henriques Street in tribute to Basil Henriques, OBE (1948) who died on 2nd December 1961, and was the founder of the Bernhard Baron Oxford and St George Settlement, a youth club for lads in the area which he opened on 3rd March 1914, when he was 24. The street leads southwards from Commercial Road, not far east of its junction with Whitechapel Road, and was named Berner Street on 1st May 1868, being an amalgamation of Upper Berner Street, Lower Berner Street, and Batty Buildings. In the 1880s this street was regarded as 'respectable' and was inhabited by people who worked as dock labourers, carmen and shoe-makers. There were also several tailors. A public house called the George IV at No. 68, on the corner of Boyd Street, was managed by Edmund Farrow, and the Nelson Beer House, run by Louis Hagens at No. 46, on the corner of Fairclough Street, was three doors away from the murder site of Liz Stride. Dotted down this residential street were a few retailers such as Edwin Sumner at No. 2, just in from Commercial Road, with his greengrocers shop, and down the other end of the street at No. 74, Jacob Lubin ran another grocers store on the corner of Everard Street. Henry Norris, at No. 48, on the opposite corner to the Nelson, was a chandler, while the bakery on the corner of Boyd Street, No. 70, was run by Louis Friedman. Right down at the southern end, the last building housed the chemist shop run by John Simkin. Strangely, all these stores were on the western side of the street, which was also the side where the Ripper murdered

Berner Street in 1909, entrance to Dutfield's Yard indicated by cartwheel

his presumed third victim, Long Liz Stride. Her throat was deeply cut, but she was not otherwise mutilated, and because of this it is generally thought that the Ripper was interrupted in his work... The actual site of the murder was inside a gateway leading to Dutfields Yard, between the third and fourth houses from the corner where the Nelson stood. The building on the north side of the yard (No. 40) housed the International Working Men's Educational Club, a high-flown name for what was basically a well-known, and locally disliked, radical hangout. There were many witnesses called to testify from this street. From No. 14 - Mrs. Rosenfield and, possibly, her sister, Mrs. Eva Harstein (though she may have lived in Dutfield's Yard itself): No. 28 - Abraham Ashbrigh (or Heahbury as reported in the papers) (17): No. 30 – Charles Letchford (22): No. 36 - Mrs. Fanny Mortimer (48): No. 38 - Barnett Kentorrich: No. 44 - Matthew Packer (59), the general dealer who allegedly sold grapes to Long Liz sometime before her murder, and at No. 64 - William Marshall (47). It is interesting to note that in 1891, living at No. 70, is 28-year-old master-baker, Maurice Kosminski!

Dutfield's Yard: This is only known as such because of the main business carried on there by Arthur Dutfield, who was a cart and van manufacturer. The people who actually lived in the yard were listed in the 1891 census as living at 40 Berner Street (in Stable Yard). This house, although listing several residents (whether they were living there permanently is not clear), was the headquarters of the IWMEC – as noted above.

Mitre Square: This was the site of the fourth in the Ripper's acknowledged series of five murders and the death of Catherine Eddowes. It is generally assumed that it was in total frustration at having been interrupted at the Berner Street site that the Ripper struck again so soon afterwards - a mere three quarters of an hour later. Mitre Square was the only murder site not within the jurisdiction of the Metropolitan CID as it stood inside the boundaries of the City of London, and this led to more complications of delegation as the case was suddenly open to a whole new section of the police force. Mitre Square was a small enclosed area between Mitre Street on the west and Duke Street to the east, and could only be reached by three alleys - Church Passage, leading from Duke Street, an unnamed passage leading northwards into St James Place and a twenty-five foot roadway leading in from Mitre Street itself. The square was mainly surrounded by warehouses: the area between Church Passage and the unnamed passage, the north-eastern corner was covered by a large block owned by tea and coffee merchants Heseltine, Kearley and Tonge, then sandwiched between another Kearley and Tonge warehouse and a large block occupied by Walter Williams and Co. On the corner of Mitre Street, two old houses remained from an earlier era, one of which (No. 3) was occupied by PC Richard Pearce (serving with the City of London Police Force) and his family. After the entrance from Mitre Street, there was a row of four houses – all empty, though picture-frame maker C Taylor & Co had business premises at Nos. 8/9 - No. 9 being on the corner leading into Mitre Square. A small passageway and yard separated the backs of these houses from the last large warehouse in the square belonging to Horner and Co. and it was in the corner behind the house next to Mr. Taylor, number 8 Mitre Street - that Catherine Eddowes' body was found by PC Edward Watkins. The square is still in place today, but all the surrounding buildings have been rebuilt in the last thirty or so, years, and it is now a relatively ugly, but peaceful, backwater where office workers eat their luncheon sandwiches on sunny days, some sitting on the edge of the bed of flowers that now stands where Mr. Taylor once framed his pictures.

13 Miller's Court: The last murder site and site of the only indoor killing. Miller's Court was a small enclosed area surrounded by small, mean houses, and with no other exit but the very narrow passageway leading between Nos. 26 and 27 into the north side of Dorset Street, a narrow, sordid and dangerous back street exiting into the west side of Commercial Street, almost opposite the notorious Fashion Street. It was in this small room, partitioned off from the front of No. 26 and designated No. 13, and which was only accessible through a door on the right-hand side of the passage to the court, that Mary Jane Kelly became the last accepted victim of Jack the Ripper in his most horrific crime, after which he completely disappeared. It is not clear whether John McCarthy (37 years in 1888) actually owned No. 27 (although he implies it in his original statement to the police after the discovery of Mary Kelly's body), but he certainly had lived there all through the 1880s with his wife Elizabeth, 36, and children, John Jr, 14, still at school, Margaret, 12 and Elizabeth who was 9. His brother, Daniel, lived with them also, and later ran a grocers store in competition with his brother at No. 36 Dorset Street. Over the decade of the '80s the occupants of No. 26 dwindled from thirteen at the beginning, to a mere two at the turn into the '90s.

Dorset Street: Running west to east from Crispin Street to Commercial Street, exiting opposite 'Itchy Park' (the disused graveyard of Christ Church), this was said to be one of the most notorious and dangerous streets in the Whitechapel/Spitalfields area, where police officers, even in pairs, would only go if absolutely necessary. It was given its name on 22nd November 1867 and was a short, narrow and tawdry street, which, by the 1880s, was almost entirely taken up with lodging and doss houses - in fact there were only two legitimate businesses listed in the *Post Office Street Directory* for 1888: Barnett Price had a grocery store at No. 7, while further along the northern side the Blue Coat Boy public house was run by William James Turner at No. 32. It was estimated that on any one night there were no fewer than 1,200 men sleeping in these cramped and sordid quarters. The street also seems to be central to the Whitechapel Murders as many people connected to the case lived there or had some other connection with it. John Stedman has recently identified Crossingham's Lodging House as being situated at No. 15, on the south side of the street, right opposite the entrance to Miller's Court and not, as has been previously assumed by most enthusiasts (myself included), on the eastern corner of Little Paternoster Row at number 35. Miller's Court led off the north side between Nos. 26 and 27, about a third of the way down from the Britannia Beer House on the corner of Commercial Street which was managed at this time by Matilda Ringer, and was consequently known as 'Mrs. Ringers', her husband having died in July 1881. At the other end of the street was another hostelry called The Horn of Plenty at no 5 Crispin Street which several authors have mistaken for the Britannia, and whose proprietor in 1888 was one Christopher Bowen. At this time public houses had to be licensed, but beer could be sold anywhere without the need for licensing. A photograph of this pub exists taken in about 1912 - but no one seems to have discovered it. The western end of Dorset Street was exactly opposite the Providence Row Night Refuge and Convent which stood at 50 Crispin Street, and was still carrying on its charitable work until recently. Now it is under renovation and conversion. Dorset Street was renamed Duval Street on 28th June 1904, but if it was changed because of the notoriety brought about by the famous murder of Mary Jane Kelly, the council certainly took their time to do so! The northern side of the street was demolished in 1928 to make room for enlargements to Spitalfields Market, with the southern side being cleared in the 1960s leaving what was once Dorset/Duval Street as merely an unnamed service road beside a multi-storey car park. An ignominious end for so notorious a street, but possibly well-earned.

26 Dorset Street: This was the house in which Mary Kelly rented the partitioned-off back room designated 13 Miller's Court.

27 Dorset Street: John McCarthy owned this house and had his chandlery shop there, although he was only listed for the first time in *Kelly's Post Office Trade Directory* as a chandler in 1890. He presumably owned or leased No. 26, and possibly the houses actually in Miller's Court as these were locally known as 'McCarthy's Rents'.

30 Dorset Street: The address at which Amelia Farmer (sometimes known as Palmer) lived for four years. She was Annie Chapman's friend and gave evidence at her inquest. Annie herself had lived at this address in 1886 with a man called Jack Sivvey, or Siffey, by which name Annie was also sometimes known.

35 Dorset Street: This has always been thought to be the address of Crossingham's Lodging House, but in 1997 John Stedman placed Crossingham's at No. 15 Dorset Street having done extensive research into the history of the street. No. 35 may very well have been an annexe or extension also owned or run by Crossingham, and was situated on the eastern corner of Paternoster Row, a small alley/street which ran northwards into Brushfield Street. *The Jack the Ripper A-Z* states that from about May 1888 Annie Chapman lived mainly at this address until she died. Pearly Poll, the friend of Martha Tabram, also lived here for a while, as did Elizabeth Allen and Eliza Cooper, both of whom gave evidence at Martha's inquest.

38 Dorset Street: The press reported inaccurately that Michael Kidney said he lived at this address with Elizabeth Stride. Kidney in fact said that they lived together at 35 Devonshire Street.

The Commercial Street Public Houses (from north to south)

The Commercial Tavern: An attractive example of Victorian architecture, this pub is smaller inside than it appears from the outside. Its rounded façade stands on the corner of a small side street called Wheller Street (the same name today, though there's not much of it left!) A pub never, to my knowledge, connected to the

Jack the Ripper case, although it stands directly opposite what was in 1888 the Commercial Street Police Station, and must have been frequented, I have no doubt, by many local officers involved in the case.

The Golden Heart: Standing on the southern corner of Hanbury Street at its intersection with Commercial Street, this Truman's pub is now a comparatively modern building dating from the 1930s, and although it stands not more than 300 yards from the site of Annie Chapman's death is another pub that has never, to my knowledge, been connected to the case of Jack the Ripper, or even mentioned with regard to any of the participants. Its most interesting connection is that just around the corner at 12 Hanbury Street a certain Bud Flanagan was born on 14 October 1896 (see: Hanbury Street).

The Red Lion: This pub at 92 Commercial Street was a beer house owned in 1888 by Frederick Garner & Co, although they were only landlords for two years. The pub had no known connection to the Ripper murders, although it is more than likely that some of the victims drank there at some time. It ceased being a pub in 1926 when Simon Cohen moved in with his paper bag manufacturing business. It was on the north corner of Red Lion Court which became Puma Court on 11 July 1893.

The Ten Bells: On the north-eastern corner of Church Street (now Fournier Street) and Commercial Street stood the Ten Bells public house, adjacent to Hawksmoor's Christchurch, with its adjoining cemetery known in the 1880s as 'Itchy Park'. There has been a public house on this site since at least 1752 (and possibly since before 1715). In 1976 it was renamed the Jack the Ripper in a bid to cash in on the notorious reputation of the area. It caused something of a furore amongst the feminist movement who eventually managed to get the name reverted to the Ten Bells.

Elizabeth Foster told the press that she had been drinking here with Mary Kelly on 8 November - the evening before she was murdered. She also cast doubt on the testimony of Maria Harvey in a statement published in the *Evening News* dated 12 November 1888. This pub has recently been bought for an estimated £1 million

(February 2002) and renovated, cleaned up and generally made more comfortable, with a special 'Ripper' room on the first floor, and is an essential place to visit for anyone interested in the Whitechapel murders, or even only in the history of the East End.

The Britannia: As this establishment was only entitled to sell beer, it was not entered on the contemporary Ordnance Survey maps as a public house, but it stood on the north corner of Commercial Street and Dorset Street, and in 1888 was run by Matilda Ringer and was consequently popularly known as "Mrs. Ringer's". The Britannia was demolished in 1928 along with the rest of the north side of Dorset Street, (including Miller's Court) when Spitalfields Market was being extended. It has sometimes been confused by certain researchers with The Horn of Plenty which stood at the opposite end of Dorset Street facing the Provident Row Convent and Night Refuge at 50 Crispin Street - a building which is still standing, although it is at present being renovated and converted, presumably for high-quality residential dwellings (February 2002). Mary Kelly was known to drink at this establishment.

The Queen's Head: On the north corner of Fashion Street, where it enters Commercial Street stood the Queen's Head. The building is still there today but is not open to the public. Charles Preston said in his testimony that Elizabeth Stride had been arrested here about four or five months before her death, and she also drank here with Elizabeth Tanner on the eve of her death. It was outside this pub that George Hutchinson said he'd leant on a lamppost and watched Mary Kelly being picked up by a stranger, who he later described in such minute detail that one is led to be suspicious of his statement.

The Princess Alice (now The City Darts [1996]): This pub is situated on the south-eastern corner of Wentworth Street where it crosses Commercial Street. It was allegedly frequented by the suspect known as 'Leather Apron', and it was also here that Frances Coles (Carrotty Nell) was picked up by Thomas Sadler who was suspected of her murder on 14 February 1891.

Commercial Street in 1905, with the Britannia on the left and the Ten Bells, right

Other Streets in the Whitechapel Area

Aldgate East Station: This station was opened on 6 October 1884, and was on the District Railway extension from Mansion House to New Cross Gate. The present station is not on the original site, having been moved several hundred metres further east when the triangular junction at Aldgate was being enlarged. The new, and present, siting was opened on 31 October 1938. The original designated name for the station was Commercial Road, but the station sadly no longer carries any of its original design features, although there are some interesting details surviving from the 1938 re-design, notable the rare silver roundels with infill lettering which are above the two stairway entrances.

Angel Alley: A narrow passage passing from Whitechapel High Street to Wentworth Street and next to George Yard on its eastern side (where Martha Tabram was murdered on 7th August 1888). This seems to have been the most salubrious street in this drab area in the mid 1800s, and was dominated by 'bad houses'. John Hollingshead reports in the first of 10 articles he wrote for the *Morning Post* under the overall title of 'London Horrors', starting on 21 January 1861 (and thereafter daily, except Sunday), that they were "the cleanest looking houses in the district" and that the "windows have tolerably neat green blinds, the doors have brass plates, and inside the houses there is comparative comfort, if not plenty". This relatively high standard was evidently afforded mainly by the custom of farmer's men who supplied the Whitechapel Hay Market twice weekly. At the left hand side of the entrance to this alley stood the Angel Public House (strangely enough!), whose proprietor was one Henry Burgess in 1888, and on the right side, Henry Randell was in residence as a hosier.

Baker's Row (now Vallance Road): This was originally a narrow roadway leading northwards from Whitechapel Road to an odd junction at the corner of Church Street (which became part of Hanbury Street in 1879), where it became Charles Street which was incorporated into Baker's Row when it was later widened. Eventually the whole road was given the new name of Vallance Road on 21 January 1896. It was at the corner of Baker's Row and Hanbury Street that the two carmen, Charles Cross and Robert Paul found PC Jonas Mizen who they told about their discovery of a body in Bucks Row - the body later found to be that of Polly Nichols.

Breezer's Hill: This was where Mary Kelly was believed to have lived for a year or so from 1885 at number 1 - the house of John (a dock labourer) and Mary McCarthy. It is pretty obvious that the newspapers quoting 'Mrs. Carthy' had misheard her name - Carthy being an extremely rare name in the area. Breezer's Hill was a short street of about 80 metres at the west end of Pennington Street and ran northwards uphill to St George's Street (once the notorious Ratcliff Highway - today, just The Highway) which itself was a little south of the Swedish Church in Prince's Square where Liz Stride had registered as an unmarried woman on 10th July 1866. Pennington Street ran east-west along London Docks North Quay (it still does) not very far east of the Tower of London and the south side was taken up with drug and cotton warehouses - now News International. The house in which Mary had stayed was greatly overshadowed by the huge bulk of the new wool warehouse built in 1884 which took up the entire western side of the street and housed the company of Gooch and Cousens. At one time there was a pub at each end of this short street - at the top on the eastern corner stood the White Bear at No. 1 St George Street, where Mary Kelly most certainly would have drunk while Paul Carl Richard Cross was the landlord in 1885, and at the bottom end, with no number, had been the Red Lion, but this was long demolished by the time Mary lived in Breezer's Hill - had she done so - the last proprietor before it closed in 1874 being a John Salter.

Church Street (now Fournier Street): Ending at Brick Lane at the east, it was named because it ran alongside Hawksmoor's Christchurch from the Ten Bells pub on the Commercial Street end. The small graveyard beside this church was known in the 1880s as 'Itchy Park' and was a crowded haunt of tramps, vagrants, down-and-outs, prostitutes and drunks. It was at the Ten Bells that Mary Kelly had been reported by the press as drinking with Elizabeth Foster on 8 November 1888 - the evening before she was murdered. The order for the change of name to Fournier Street, which it is still called today, was made on 7 November 1893. It is a street of beautiful Huguenot houses built in the 18th century which are now being renovated.

Commercial Road: In the mid 1800s this was one of the widest streets in London and was built to facilitate transport to and from the London Docks. Being a major thoroughfare for wagon transportation it was laid with stone tramways on each side of the road going as far as Blackwall. This road is the link between several streets connected to the Whitechapel murders - most notably Berner Street, where the body of Liz Stride was found. The next street moving eastwards is Batty Street, where another murder was committed – that of Miriam Angel by Israel Lipski in June 1887 at No. 16, and also living along this street at the time of the Whitechapel murders was Francis Tumblety, the Littlechild suspect, at No. 22. Several hundred yards eastward there were two dismal streets of peripheral interest - Star Street, where it was incorrectly reported that Martha Tabram lived with William Turner, and right next to that was Devonshire Street where Liz Stride had lived with Michael Kidney. Settles Street ran northwards off this major thoroughfare just opposite Christian Street and was where Liz Stride and a stranger had been mocked by three men as they kissed and cuddled in the rain outside the Bricklayers Arms, run by Walter Cook.

Devonshire Street (became Winterton Street, now demolished): A small street leading southwards off Commercial Road several hundred yards east of Berner Street, (a little south of the London Hospital, and almost opposite Sidney Street - itself to become famous with the Siege in 1911) where Liz Stride had lived with Michael Kidney for several years at No. 35 until about five months before her death, when they moved to No. 36 - no reason is known for this move. This street was next to Star Street on the eastern side (where some papers said Mrs. Bousfield had her lodging house, but this was actually in Star Place, at the bottom end of the street). Its name was changed on 29 July 1890 to Winterton Street, and, of course, it no longer exists today - the site of both these streets now being covered by the amazingly horrendous Watney Market. After taking Star Street as representative of the parish of St George-in-the-East and describing its squalor at length in his study published as Ragged London in 1861, John Hollingshead says of Devonshire Street that it was "...as full of hunger, dirt and social degradation as Star Street..." The census taken on 6 February 1861 notes that "...in this street and in Star Street there are living in 123 houses about 1,500 persons, including 300 children, many without shoes or stockings...". The average rent per room for a week was 1s 9d with the lowest rent in this area being attributed to Friendly Place (regarded as "...low..." inhabitant-wise) whereas the highest recorded rent was 4s 0d in Sutton Street ("...a few respectable inhabitants and lodgers..."). The poverty in these streets is scarcely believable today and it would hardly have changed in the intervening years to 1888 - life moved considerably slower at that time.

Fairclough Street: This street was originally another North Street which was changed to its present name on the 26th November 1869. It was outside the Beehive Tavern, standing on the corner of Christian Street, that Diemschutz and Kozebrodski found the horse-keeper called Edward Spooner (not the policeman they were hoping to find) who they took back to Dutfield's Yard after the discovery of Liz Stride's body. On the corner of Berner Street, three doors away from the yard, Louis Hagens was the landlord of the Nelson Beer House, which was numbered 46 Berner Street. This corner building is beautifully shown in the picture (taken on 7 April 1909) published in Melvyn Fairclough's book (another coincidence!) *The Ripper and the Royals* (1991), as is Matthew Packer's shop next door - though it is hard to picture that facade as a shop.

Fashion Street, Flower and Dean Street, Thrawl Street: The few acres that these streets covered have been demolished and built over, the new Toynbee Estate being opened in 1984 by Prince Charles. Fashion Street is still a complete street but in 1888 was full of cheap and sordid doss houses and had a notorious reputation. The Queen's Head pub stood on the northern corner with Commercial Street and it was where George Hutchinson alleged he saw Mary Kelly being picked up by a stranger the night she was murdered. Only the entrance from Commercial Street still survives to show where Flower and Dean Street once lay, although the name is commemorated in a Flower and Dean Walk. Lolesworth Street (once George Street) has now completely disappeared, though what little is left of Flower and Dean Street is actually now named Lolesworth Close - confusing? Yes! Thrawl Street itself has also completely gone, though the exit into Brick Lane beside what was once the Frying Pan Public House (now the Sheraz Restaurant - Balti Cuisine!) is still called Thrawl Street. In reality, today's Thrawl Street is a road winding through the new estate. At the entrance from Wentworth Street stands an arch which was originally sited on Rothschild Buildings in Flower and Dean Street, on which is written: 'Erected by the Four Per Cent Industrial Dwellings Company Ltd - 1886'.

32 Flower and Dean Street (now demolished): Elizabeth Stride was an occasional lodger at this address from 1882 onwards, and Catherine Lane, a charwoman who had been friendly with Stride for six or seven years, had lived here since 11 February 1888 and said that Long Liz had moved in on 27 September after a row with Michael Kidney, with whom she had lived until then. The street was parallel to, and in between, Fashion Street to the north and Thrawl Street to the south, all running eastwards from Commercial Street to Brick Lane.

52 Flower and Dean Street (now demolished): The White House was a doss house that allowed men and women to sleep together. This was the house where Polly Nichols was staying when she was murdered on 31 August 1888. In *The Victorian Underworld* by Kellow Chesney there is an excellent description of the initiation or training of a "tooler" (pickpocket) by two "kidsmen" who lived with their mistresses, each occupying a complete floor of a house in this street. The income from this "trade" must have been considerable for the area. The main targets for their attention were wealthy ladies of certain class who would shop at the fashionable St Paul's Churchyard with their voluminous crinolines making it easy to slip a hand in their pockets without being detected.

18 George Street (now demolished): Emma Elizabeth Smith, who was attacked on Osborn Street and died of her wounds on 5 April 1888, lived at this address. Rose Mylett, who was found dead in Clarke's Yard at 4.15am on 20 December 1888, had also lived here on occasions. This street ran from Flower and Dean Street to Wentworth Street passing through Thrawl Street, and at some time before 1894 the name was changed to Lolesworth Street. In the 1980s this whole area was razed and a new complex of modern house was laid out destroying the original plan of streets.

19 George Street (now demolished): Satchell's Lodging House - where, on 20 November 1888, Annie Farmer had said she had been attacked by a "client" who she accused of being Jack the Ripper. This was also where Martha Tabram had been living at the time of her death on 7 August 1888.

Wickam's of Mile End Road: About halfway between Whitechapel and Stepney Green tube stations on the north side of Mile End Road stands an interesting edifice, originally built as Wickam's Department Store. Speigelhalter Bros, the jewellers at No. 81, refused to sell their lease, so the store was built around the shop with the intention of building over No. 81 at a later date. This never happened, and today one can see the building with this small, bleak house right in the middle of the grandiose department store, looking very forlorn. Wickam's closed its doors in the 1960s, but the Speigelhalters (who were Christian Moravians from Germany) stayed on. (Is there a lesson to be learnt here?!)

Star Street (became Planet Street, now demolished): Star Street was a little over half a mile along Commercial Road and led southwards (parallel to Berner Street). There seems to be some confusion as to whether Mrs. Bousfield lived in Star Street or Star Place, but it was, in fact, Star Place. The history of this street is also a little muddled, and it seems it was originally designated Planet Street, but became Star Street on 23 June 1865, though this name was abolished on 15 December 1891 when it reverted to Planet Street. Star Street was comprised of 63 two-up, two-down houses, renting in 1861 for an average of 1s 9d and being home for 252 families, the average room size was 9'5" x 9'5", with the height being a mere 8'5". Along with Devonshire Street, it has long since vanished in the 1960s demolition spree. John Hollingshead, taking this street as representative of the parish of St George-in-the-East, describes it in great detail in his *Ragged London* in 1861: "Its road is black and muddy, half filled with pools of inky water...." He goes on to describe a room which is inhabited by a chimney sweep with two women, an infant and two young children "...playing on the black floor...eating what is literally bread and soot...". Two other rooms held nine dwellers, and two more held eleven each, all in the utmost squalor and poverty. Today this is hard to believe, yet things cannot have improved much in the twenty-five odd years between then and when Martha Tabram and Henry Turner were living in Star Place in 1888.

Star Place (now demolished): The Bousfield family rather dominated this short cul-de-sac of just six houses in the 1880s. In 1881 at No. 2 was carman Benjamin Bousfield (32) with his wife Ann, four years his junior, three sons (Benjamin Jr, 11, William, 4, and Thomas, 2) and his nine-year-old daughter, Ann. Then just along at No. 4 was William Bousfield, a chopper of firewood, with his wife Mary, with their namesake daughter of five and one-year-old son James. The street was a small alley running east/west at the bottom of Star Street itself, and it is more than likely that Martha Tabram and William Turner would have drunk at The Star while living with the Bousfields in 1888, it being their nearest local, at No. 2 Morris Street on the corner of Star Place, and managed at this time by William Harris. They very probably knew and drank with Liz Stride and Michael Kidney who lived for several years in Devonshire Street (the next street, parallel to Star Street on the eastern side). By 1891 there were no Bousfields at number 2, but another branch was installed at number 3. Another carman, James, 31, and his wife, Mary (a popular name in this family!), just a year his junior, with their children, Sarah, 7, Charlotte, 2, and newborn Maude, at merely a few months. Martha Tabram and William Turner's erstwhile landlords were still at No. 4 with their rapidly expanding brood which had the additions of Bella, 10, William, 8, Ben, 7, and little George, now, 5.

Winthrop Street (now demolished): The street was parallel to Bucks Row where Harrison, Barber & Co. Ltd had their horse-slaughtering premises on the south side at Nos. 19, 21 and 23, and where Harry Tomkins, James Mumford and Charles Britten (or Brittain) worked, who became the first people of the "general public" to view the body of Polly Nichols after its discovery by

Charles A Cross and Robert Paul at about 3.45am on 31st August 1888. Previously the street was known as Little North Street but the name was changed to Winthrop Street on 12 October 1883 - just five years before the Ripper commenced his atrocities in the next street, Buck's Row. In 1881 James Barber lived at No. 2, with his wife, Mary, two sons and three servants, but by 1891 he had move along to No. 19 with a second wife, Emily, a new son, and now a daughter, and also a step-son, two servants and a nurse. Further along the street at No. 22 was now living James Mumford, one of the first three to see Polly Nichols' body, as mentioned above.

1997

"PICTURES, PAINT, AND PROSCENIUMS"
A Brief Biography of the Artist William D Stewart

ANDY ALIFFE

This article appeared in edition number 14 of Ripperologist

William Stewart's book *Jack the Ripper: A New Theory*, is a scarce, and much sought-after early Ripper work. Published in 1939, it is the third English language book on the subject in the 20th Century, following Leonard Matters' *The Mystery of Jack the Ripper* (1929) and Edwin T Woodhall's *Jack the Ripper or When London Walked in Terror* (1935). Stewart's "*New Theory* explores the then controversial theme that 'Jack' could have been 'Jill' - an idea suggested by Sir Arthur Conan Doyle at an earlier date.

Stewart asked these questions:

What sort of person could be out at night without exciting the suspicion of the household or neighbours, who were keyed up with suspicion on account of the mysterious crimes?

What sort of person could pass through the streets without exciting suspicion? What sort of person could have the elementary anatomical knowledge which was evidenced by the mutilations, and the skill to perform them in a way as to make some people think a doctor was responsible? What sort of person could have risked being found by the dead body, yet have a perfect alibi?

Stewart concluded that it was a woman who was or who had been a midwife.

The *Jack the Ripper A-Z* says the book is easily under-rated, but Stewart's theory, that an abortionist-midwife, who killed Kelly while she was pregnant, "has fallen with the discovery of Dr. Bond's report... which shows that she was NOT pregnant".

After many months of research and dead ends, including finding the wrong William Stewart (with East End and Ripper connections!), I finally tracked down the right one and spent a delightful day in West Sussex, with his daughter Jean Coram and grandson Breck. Jean, now in her eighties, is a sprightly lady, living in Bohemian splendor in the family home of many years. She followed in her father "Doogie's", footsteps, studying art, design and sculpture at the same Lambeth art college attended by William in the early 1900s. indeed it was Jean that designed and drew the now familiar picture on the Quality Street chocolate boxes and tins. Jean's son Breck is also a portrait artist, and has had financial success painting and selling pictures of classic American cars.

William Douglas Stewart was born in Greenwich in July 1883. He was the son of Douglas Stewart, an author and play-wright, and the grandson of Alexander Stewart, the celebrated Arabic scholar.

At the age of twenty, William was Advertising Director of the London Press Exchange, commissioning pen and ink artwork for the many Fleet Street illustrated papers. William himself was also drawing satirical cartoons for *Punch* during this period. As a jobbing author and artist, he was a freelance illustrator, when times were hard, and spent a couple of years writing a different short story every day for the *Evening Standard*.

He was proud of his Scottish heritage, and a follower of the emerging Suffragette Movement, leading a Pipe Band to the gates of Holloway Prison in May 1921 when Sylvia Pankhurst was released. It was during this time he developed his great interest and life-long passion that would eventually became a full time occupation - theatrical scenic design.

In the First World War he was based in Wales as an official war artist, representing the *Illustrated London News*. He was made a member of the British Watercolour Society in 1918 and of the RBA in 1924. On two occasions, he had a painting on the line at the Royal Academy.

At the end of WW1, he became a full-time scenic designer for the Stoll Variety Theatre chain. Jean remembers with youthful enthusiasm her early school days, travelling to the many theatres around the country, spending years at a time in Aberdeen, Edinburgh and Liverpool, living in theatrical digs with all the associated stories and characters. The family eventually headed back south when Doogie's scenic work brought him to the Elephant and Castle Theatre, run by the ever-popular Tod Slaughter.

Tod and William's association and friendship grew over the time they were at the "Elephant". The highlights of William's work were Tod Slaughter's Christmas pantomimes. They caused gasps of delight and applause from audiences, and Slaughter often persuaded William to take a bow on stage in recognition of his work.

Jean remembered "Old Slaughter" paying local characters a couple of pounds a night to be extras in some of the big pantomime scenes, all of whom were given star treatment by hoots and cheers from friends and family in the audience. She also remembered that audiences could be over-enthusiastic. One time, she and her mother were in the theatre on an opening night to see one of her father's great transformation scenes, but just as the curtain was rising, her mother was hit on the head by a sweet thrown from the upper-circle 'gods'. She passed out and had to be carried from the theatre, with the "tragedy" making the local paper a few days later under the headline "Lady hit on head by Pear-Drop"!

William formed a friendship with Sir Frank Brangwyn, the noted decorative painter and sculptor, during this period. They shared an interest in the legends, buildings, folklore, and characters of the East End, and spent many months between them, sketching and photographing the cockney community, laying the foundations for two of Stewart's future books.

A new type of theatre was beginning to emerge and Stewart's scenic work was becoming seasonal, so he returned to advertising as Production Manager with the British Commercial Gas Association. Indeed, Jean wrote and illustrated a children's book for the company, based on "Mr. Therm", as suggested by another artist and friend, Eric Gill.

By now the idea of the Jack the Ripper book was beginning to take shape. William had already painted a series of East End scenes, and had shown the collection as a one-man show. But now he returned to photograph what then remained of the Ripper sites.

Jean would often accompany her father on his East End sorties, posing for the outlines of the victims' bodies tor William's photographic reconstructions and she also unknowingly contributed to the model sets. On one occasion her father needed a scaled paisley shawl for a model of one of the victims and Jean was horrified to find that he had, during the night, cut off the end of her boyfriend's favourite paisley tie!

As a keen amateur photographer (he wrote a book called *Profitable Amateur Photography*!) Doogie developed his own films and was rather shaken one time when, in 1938, a developing picture of a front window of 29 Hanbury Street produced an image of a woman in working class Victorian clothes. This caused a certain amount of excitement when he sent it to the Psychical Research Society, but no satisfactory answer was ever given as to its origin. Stewart spent many months researching the then known facts concerning the Whitechapel murders, consulting several officers who were engaged on the killings at the time.

His set-designing abilities were used to great effect throughout his book, providing reconstructions of some of the murder sites. Early in 1938, the *Evening News* began running a series of articles on "Murder Street", identified as Duval Street (Dorset Street) and Miller's Court. William sent the editor a photograph of his model reconstruction of Mary Kelly's room, and as luck would have it, a senior Scotland Yard official was there when it arrived. So convincing was its likeness that the inspector wanted to know how

William Stewart's model of Mary Kelly's room

"Mr. Stewart was able to obtain details which as far as he knew were only available at the Yard?" Obviously William's contacts had given and shown him privileged information.

Jack the Ripper was published in March 1939 amid the usual reviews, several picking up on the "New Theory" - that of a woman killer - as similar to Mrs. Pearcy, of the Camden Town murder of 1890. The book even attracted comment from the *Times Literary Supplement* saying 'The verb 'to peeve' and 'to contact' do not exist in reputable English and the split infinitives on page 213 require at least an apology"! It also goes on to congratulate Stewart for his "experiments in reconstructing the crimes free from the terror and disarray which they provoked among contemporary commentators".

Stewart had re-staged the murder of Catherine Eddowes in Mitre Square to prove that the night watchman who said he heard nothing must have been wrong. Stewart tore a piece of apron cloth which echoed around the Mitre Square buildings.

The *Times Literary Supplement* also makes mention on the cynical reflections, quoted in the book, of Mr. George Bernard Shaw. William Stewart took the trouble of sending GBS his proof copy for comment. Shaw returned the manuscript, annotated in his own handwriting, but none too pleased!

There were plans to turn the book into a film, but with the outbreak of the Second World War these plans were shelved. After the war, William's easel works of the theatre, a record of his life's work, were exhibited around the country under the title of "Fifty Years Back Stage" and they were the subject of a four-page feature by the *Illustrated London News*.

An introduction to this exhibition says "The theatre, in its widest sense, has stimulated many famous artists to produce some of their finest works, the names of Degas and Toulouse-Lautrec springing readily to mind. Today the photographer finds ballet and the theatre attractive and challenging subjects, for the employment of his skills. There can have been very few artists, however, who have attempted to record the more intimate life of the theatre, the scenes behind the scenes, the people who make the theatre function and the techniques used by the producer and stage manager. William Stewart has found a wealth of fascinating. subjects for the sketches which he enjoyed doing - the property man, stage hands, the effects equipment, the trials and tribulations of the touring company - and for half a century he used his skills to record aspects of the theatre, many of which have completely disappeared".

I am happy to say that I am helping Jean to find a permanent home for this collection at Covent Garden's Theatre Museum.

William Stewart's last book, *Characters of Bygone London*, published in 1960, was a collection of sketches of Victorian and Edwardian people and long forgotten East End trades and occupations, all taken from photographs and drawings from his earlier wanderings, when he actually met, knew and became friends with these folk.

William Douglas Stewart died in 1965 aged 82.

1998
"THE FOULEST DEED OF MODERN TIMES"
A Re-evaluation of the Jack the Ripper Contemporary Literature

ADAM WOOD

This article appeared in edition number 15 of Ripperologist

Andy Aliffe's brilliantly-researched article on William Stewart in December 1997's *Ripperologist* stated that *Jack the Ripper - A New Theory* was the third 20th century Ripper book in the English language after Matters and Woodhall. This prompted me to look up how many titles had been published before that in the aftermath of the murders at the end of the 19th century. It's a staggering fact that Stewart's book was one of the first dozen, and some fifty-odd have been published since then, "some good, the majority atrocious" to quote Philip Sugden.

These early publications, some emerging while the crimes were still taking place, have long been seen as being of little value except for collectability, the information contained within dismissed as inaccurate and sensationalist.

It is indeed true that some are little more than a collection of second-hand reports and misconceptions. Another reading of these books, however, turns up plenty or food for thought. General questions raised by a re-evaluation of the contemporary literature include the cover of *The Whitechapel Murders: Or, the Mysteries of the East End*, published before the murder of Mary Kelly. A reward poster lists the (then) four victims, number one being 'unknown', killed on 4 December 1887. The details given inside make it clear Emma Smith is being referred to, but why 4th December? Is this a possible source for the Fairy Fay 'myth'? It's also interesting to note the address of the publishers of this account: G Purkess, 286 Strand - three doors away from Grand and Batchelor, the private investigators involved in the case of Elizabeth Stride. It would seem possible the two parties were known to each other; indeed the detectives get a glowing write-up on page 43!

Even the name Jack the Ripper is treated in such a way as to make for some thought-provoking observations. In the last issue of *Ripperologist* (issue 14), in my review of *The Jack the Ripper Whitechapel Murders* by Andy and Sue Parlour, I gave three sources for reason to believe the name may have been in use before the 'Dear Boss' letter was published. These were the diary entry by Johannis Palmer, a letter published for the first time in Paul Feldman's *The Final Chapter*, and Walter Dew's *The Hunt for Jack the Ripper* (p117/118).

Philip Sugden, in *The Complete History of Jack the Ripper* (pbk p121), suggests Dew's memory was at fault as the name had not been invented yet. This would be true if the name had been invented specifically for the 'Dear Boss' letter dated 25th September. However, there is absolutely no reason why the name could not have been in public use beforehand, even if the writer of the letter invented it - it might not have been committed to paper until the date of the letter.

Further sources for early use of 'Jack the Ripper' include *The Fifty Most Amazing Crimes of the Last 100 Years* (p246), in which it is stated: "On September 9th alone, twelve suspects were taken for examination to Commercial Street Police Station. During the week that followed, scores of people were detained, including William Henry Piggott, found with blood on his hands and boots after rescuing a woman from a street fight; Charles Ludwig, a German, and John Fitzgerald, who 'confessed' to an angry crowd that he was

Jack the Ripper'.

Tom Robinson's Daisy Bank Publication *Jack the Ripper* gives several interesting accounts: p15 carries a paragraph that echoes the story of Squibby given by Dew, and on p13 describes a letter signed 'Jack the Ripper' which warned of an impending murder which would take place early in September. This, Robinson states, came true with the murder of Annie Chapman. John Davis, who discovered the body, ran into the street shouting "the Ripper's been here!" (p 14). Unlikely as this and other stories may seem, it would appear unusual that so many different sources would have faulty memories when it came to reporting the use of the infamous nickname.

The most likely explanation, of course, is that these authors were writing after the event and therefore naturally later referred to the killer as 'Jack the Ripper' throughout his whole reign of terror.

The contemporary literature deals with the case of Emma Smith in much the same way as present day material: some dismiss any possibility of a link with the Ripper, some bring her up for discussion, and others simply ignore her completely. *The Whitechapel Murders, Or Mysteries of the East End* mentions the murder but says the victim was never identified, while *Leather Apron or the Horrors Of Whitechapel* tell us she was buried in Potter's Field.

Little more information is given about the murder of Martha Tabram, although Walter Dew in *The Hunt for Jack The Ripper* (p102) considers the theory at the time that the two women were victims of the same gang, possibly the High Rip Gang. Dew goes on to say that this theory was replaced by 'in all probability the correct one': that the two were victims of one man.

A couple of interesting passages regarding John Saunders Reeves and his wife are given in *The Hunt For Jack The Ripper* and *Mysteries of the East End*: Dew (p98) gives an account of Mrs. Reeves being unable to sleep due is some strange foreboding, which her husband laughed off; whilst *Mysteries* (p4) gives some fascinating information on the couple describing a menacing crowd nearby on the evening before the murder of Tabram.

By the time of Polly Nichols' murder, the contemporary press had obviously picked up on events occurring in Whitechapel. From this point forward, most of what was written is known to each of us, and equally well known are the errors which crept in. Tom Robinson, in Daisy Bank's *Jack the Ripper* (p10), said "...the reporters who visited the scenes of the Whitechapel Murders, and paid for 'special information', laid themselves open to be deceived, and much of what they wrote was sheer nonsense. No one had any information to give; everything was mere conjecture". This was undoubtedly true of much of the literature describing the murders, but some nuggets of information are there to be discovered: Emma Green stated that she could not sleep on the night of Polly Nichols' murder because she suffered from heart trouble (*History of The Whitechapel Murders*, p13). According to Walter Dew (p113), Polly's funeral procession passed down Hanbury Street the day before Annie Chapman's murder. Although it had actually happened a day earlier than remembered by Dew, this is a fair indication of the accuracy of this version of events, especially when viewing more of his statements later.

One of the most repeated 'inaccuracies' in contemporary literature is that of the graffiti on a shutter near the scene of Annie Chapman's murder. Dew (p126), *Mysteries of the East End* (p31), *The Whitechapel Murders* (Pinkerton) (p10), *History of the Whitechapel Murders* (p17) and *Leather Apron* (p9 & 54) all give accounts of the same basic message: "This is the fourth. I will murder 16 more and then give myself up". Whilst I am not suggesting that this chalked message actually existed, it is interesting to note the number of separate volumes it appeared in. I would be very interested if any reader could offer an explanation as to its origin.

Both *Mysteries of the East End* (p31) and *History of the Whitechapel Murders* (p16-17) mention two girls who stood talking in the passage of 29 Hanbury Street - who were they?

To add is this confusion, Mr. and Mrs. Copsey/Copely/Misses Huxley, *Mysteries of the East End* (p31) names Amelia Richarson's grandson as Charles Cooksley.

There are several interesting points brought up in contemporary literature regarding Eiisabeth Stride – nicknamed 'Hippy Lip Annie' in *History of the Whitechapel Murders* (p21). *Mysteries of the East End* (p45) gives a detailed insight into her dealings with the Swedish Church when reporting an interview with Sven Ollson. Ollson stated the hymn book given to Stride was an old one, published in 1821. The same interview revealed that a memorandum had been written by Rev Johannis Palmer to record the fact that Stride had been married to an Englishman. The fact that this memo was undated suggests Rev Palmer was less diligent in his record keeping than stated in Andy and Sue Parlour's *The Jack the Ripper Whitechapel Murders*.

Mysteries of the East End (p41 & 43) has plenty to say about Louis Diemschutz. At the time of Stride's murder he had been Club Steward for some six months, and on that fateful night had been returning from Westow Hill Market. The same source gives an account of how Diemschutz ran to the Club to check on the whereabouts of his wife, before lighting a candle and returning to Dutfields Yard with Kozebrodksi.

Pinkerton (p44) carries a description of the Yard itself, including three white washed cottages, written by a female reporter for a Sheffield newspaper. A small girl gives a graphic account of the discovery of Stride's body, and this source allows us a further insight of the lifestyle of the people living in Whitechapel at the time. The same reporter mentions passing a pub in Berner Street - is this the one the pipe smoker was spotted coming out of by Israel Schwartz? Has this pub ever been identified?

Perhaps the final word on Elizabeth Stride given in the contemporary literature should be made by *Leather Apron* (p14): "At Cardiff, Wales, a company of Spiritualists met and summoned the spirit of Elizabeth Stride, one of the victims. After considerable delay, which was probably caused by Elizabeth attending her toilet, so as to make herself presentable to materialize, her spirit came, and in answer to inquiries stated that her murderer was a middle-aged man, whom she mentioned by name, and who lodged, as she stated, at a certain number in Commercial Road. He belonged, she

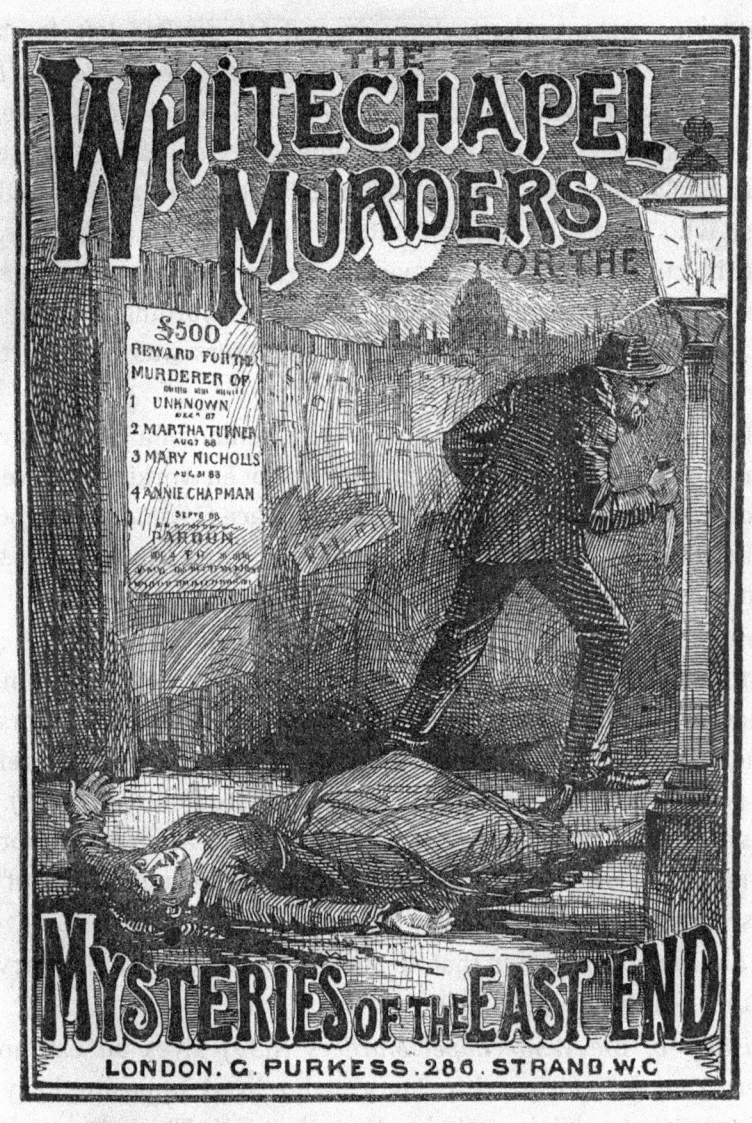

further stated, to a gang of twelve cut-throats. It is hardly necessary to add that the spirit of Elizabeth Stride was entirely off her base".

The various accounts of Catherine Eddowes' murder throw up some interesting observations: PC Watkins was talking to George Norris when they heard police whistles in the Whitechapel area:

"most probably for the Ripper" said Norris (Dew, p136).

Eddowes, apparently, had a tattooed '4' on her left forearm (*History or the Whitechapel Murders*, p22). *Mysteries of the East End* (p42) states that when her body was removed from Mitre Square, an outline in blood remained on the pavement; in view of the suggestion that an 'M' had been sawed on Catherine's face as a sign of her killer, those who advocate Francis Tumblety might be interested to read that the cuts made to her stomach were in the shape of a large 'T' (*History of the Whitechapel Murders*, p22). According to *Mysteries of the East End* (p47), one of Kate's daughters was married to a gunmaker called Phillips.

After news of her murder spread, the foreman of a gang of street cleaners came forward to say that they had been working not twenty yards from the spot where the deed took place (*Leather Apron* p67). Pinkerton (p38) gives details on possibly the first Ripper tour - two men and a woman sight-seeing in Mitre Square.

Predictably, there are many conflicting accounts of the life and death of Mary Kelly and this is still the case today. Leaving the more debatable statements to one side, there are still many points to ponder in the literature of the day. Thomas Bowyer, discoverer of the body, lived at 47 Dorset Street according to Robinson (p26). On the same page of the same source, far from being a mis-transcription of 'hair', Joe Barnett identified the body by "the peculiar shape of the ears, and colour of the eyes".

It has long been known that the name of Elizabeth Prater's cat was Diddles. Robinson (p28) tells us it was black.

History of the Whitechapel Murders (p39) gives an extremely interesting interview with 'Mary', who lived opposite Kelly in Miller's Court - this is probably Mary Ann Cox. This account gives us a much better idea of the person than any newspaper report. The same source (p34) gives Mary Jane the surname 'McCarthy', stating that her neighbours did not know her by the name Kelly.

This piece of information, although unlikely, would have been very welcome in view of the recent discovery (in 1998) of a Mary Jane Kelly born in Castletown to a woman by the name of Ann McCarthy (and the subsequent possibility that she was therefore somehow related to John McCarthy), but Robinson (p27) states that John McCarthy didn't know if she and Joe Barnett were married or not. I find it difficult to believe he wouldn't have known if indeed he was related to the victim..

I'd like to leave the final word to Tom Robinson who, on page 31 of his Daisy Bank publication, states what must have been on the minds of most people in the country at the time of the murders and in the following years: "Let's hope Britain never produced such a monster".

1999

MARY KELLY: THE (NOT SO) SIMPLE TRUTH
A Reply to John Wilding

BILL BEADLE

This article appeared in edition number 22 of Ripperologist

The question of when Mary Kelly died is to me of academic interest; no theory is based on it. 1 just began to question the orthodox version of when she died in the early seventies when l was pursuing my other great interest in crime, miscarriages of justice.

1 looked into the case of Dennis Stafford and Michael Luvagio who were gaoled in 1967 for the murder of fruit machine operator Angus Sibbet. Sibbet's dead body was found in his car at around 5.30 on a bitterly cold morning One of his car windows was wound down, another broken and snow had blown into the car. There were, therefore, similarities with 13 Miller's Court, although Sibbet's body was fully clothed, including an overcoat, not mutilated (he was shot) and he was a big man. But on the other hand, the temperature at Miller's Court was higher, there was no snow, and at 5.50am, when Sibbet's body was first medically examined, the state of rigor mortis was more advanced that at 2.00pm when Mary Kelly's body was examined.

Yet in Sibbet's case, the pathologist who conducted the autopsy decided that he had been murdered between midnight and 4.00am, favouring around 12.30am. These findings were later assessed by Prof. Francis Camps, one of the 'greats' of twentieth century pathology (and incidentally, a keen Ripperphile), who felt that insufficient attention had been paid to the likely cooling rate of the body in freezing conditions and plumped instead for 11.45pm to 2.45am, moving the likeliest time of death up to 1.30am.

Look at this in Miller's Court terms and you have 8.00am to midday, favouring 8.00am, and 8.00am to 11.00am favouring 9.30am.

l thought; "hold on - how can the time given for Mary Kelly's death be accurate?" Putting the two cases side by side - which we are entitled to do, all things being considered - then we have a much later time than Dr. Bond's subsequently revealed findings of 1.00am to 2.00am.

Bond seems to have been heavily influenced by the remains of the fish and potatoes meal in Mary's stomach:

> ...the remains of a recently taken meal were found in the stomach and scattered about over the intestines. It is therefore pretty certain that the woman must have been dead about twelve hours and the partly digested food would indicate that death took place about 3 to 4 hours after the food was taken, so 1 or 2 o'clock in the morning would be the probable time of the murder.

The problem here is that Bond, without access to modern-day knowledge, was giving the partly digested meal a much higher prominence than it merits. Currently, our most eminent pathologist is Prof. Bernard Knight, who carried out the post mortems on Fred West's victims. In *Simpson's Forensic Medicine* (eleventh edition 1997, p 25) Prof. Knight states that basing the time of death on this factor has been discredited. Knight also says that recognition of the constituents of the meal *may* (my italics) be helpful in placing the time of death soon after the meal but overall he describes the digestion process as being of very little value.

Bond appears to have based his conclusions on Mary having eaten between 9.00pm and 11.00pm on 8th November. But even if we set aside modern day reservations then where is the evidence for this assumption? Nowhere to be found. And if the police were right and she dies circa 3.30am then we have 11.30pm to 12.30am - exactly the time when she was entertaining the client with the blotchy face. Doesn't make much sense, does it? In fact the whole thing is a mish-mash of improbabilities.

We shall need to look at Bond's report again, but first I will deal with John Wilding's points in the last issue. Before examining them one by one I will make the general point that nobody who has taken issue with Mark Banner and myself has been prepared to put forward any cases which might support the 'orthodox' time of Mary's death. Bob Hinton, I am bound to say, presented an excellent overview last year, which I replied to with great pleasure because I always appreciate a well-argued case against me, but, alas, John Wilding's major points are provably wrong in every instance.

John remarks:

> *In certain people stiffening does not take place at all, while some bodies take much longer than normal to become rigid.*

Technically correct, but Professor Knight gives the precise categories of who these people are: the old, the feeble and some infants. Most emphatically not Mary Jane Kelly.

> *The bench mark for rigor mortis appears not to be sooner than three hours.*

Prof. Knight gives 1-4 hours; Prof. Donald Teare (the third member of the famous Camps-Simpson-Teare axis) 2-4 hours. Ditto Peter Dean, the country coroner for Essex and Forensic Examiner for London in *Clinical Forensic Medicine* (2nd Edition 1996 p 273), while Sir Bernard Spilsbury put forward a case in which it had set in an hour.

Well, if John wants to argue with all these *eminence grises* of the forensic profession, then so be it! We have absolutely no idea of how fierce the fire in Miller's Court was.

We only know that it was out at 2.00pm and by implication at 10.45am. As for the kettle, nobody knows when it was burnt and these matters do not help us at all. What does is Taylor's *Medical*

Dr. Thomas Bond

Jurisprudence, which tells us:

> *...a body lying exposed in a well ventilated room (eg: two broken windows) will cool more rapidly than one in a sealed room...*

As for Dr. Bond being "experienced in forensics", English forensic pathologists with specialist experience and knowledge appeared on the scene later. In 1888 Bond was the divisional police surgeon for A Division and assistant surgeon at Westminster Hospital. Nothing more. I have already dealt with the digestion process, so let us move on to the rest of Bond's findings. His report states:

...the period varies from 6-12 hours before rigidity sets in...

This is of course, wrong and so what we have is a conclusion based on two tenets, one of which is incorrect and the other highly unreliable. l must emphasise that it was not a case of Bond being incompetent but one of the standard of knowledge in 1888 being inadequate. The fallacy that rigor did not set in until 6-12 hours was still common in 1902 when it was proffered by a police surgeon in the Apted case (Harold Apted – hanged for the murder of Frances O'Rourke aged 7). ln 1999 Bond would have had a very different perspective, but in 1888 the basis on which he drew his conclusions was wrong.

Those conclusions are clearly unsound and need re-assessment. What did Bond actually find?

Rigor mortis had set in, but increased during the progress of the examination... the body was comparatively cold.

ln other words rigor was at its outset and the body comparatively cold for a corpse in that condition, which is explained by the fire being out and cool air circulating into the room making the body feel colder.

Rigor by itself is unreliable as all sources agree. Prof Knight (and Bob Hinton in his article) provides a rough guide to assist us; a body warm and flaccid has been dead less than 3 hours; warm and stiff, 3-8 hours; cold and stiff, 8-36 hours. We might also note that tissue decomposition commences in up to 50 hours and putrefaction begins to set in three or four days, depending on the environmental conditions. Hypostasis (postmortem liquidity) can set in at any time from an hour after death, normally 1-9 hours, according to Peter Dean. The latter is virtually useless in determining time of death.

It is clear from Bond's report that at 2.00pm on November 9th Mary's body was just ceasing to be fully flaccid but was comparatively cold - due to its exposure – for a body in that condition. Four hours would thus be a reasonable length of time that she had been dead.

Much beyond five hours would, in my opinion, be less and less likely as the time goes back. 9.30-10.00am would therefore be a very likely and logical time for the murder. The theory which this would mainly adversely affect would be the Maybrick theory. Between 9.30 and 10.00am accords with the witnesses who saw Mary after 8.00am that morning; Maurice Lewis between 8.00 and 8.30am and then again about an hour later, and an unnamed witness also about this time. Remember, all these times are approximate.

John Wilding states:

> *He has to kill the victim and perform complicated mutilations, which must have taken considerable time.*

Again, incorrect. There was nothing complicated about this butchery as Bond makes clear in his general assessment of the murders. Recent research strongly points to a hatchet also being used as well as a knife.

I will also deal with John's point about modus operandi, which likewise is wrong. Serial killers develop a system and pattern of actual killing although it does frequently vary from murder to murder. But they are certainly not tied to the laws of the clock. Experience shows they take their opportunities as and when they arise. Friday November 9th was a good morning for a girl to look for a bit of business as it was a holiday; plenty of punters around getting into the mood and looking to enjoy their day.

As a corollary, we should also note that Bond did not report any alcohol in Mary Kelly's body, or, apparently, the smell of it. Alcohol can linger in the body for up to a week after death - at least its smell can. Mary was reputedly tipsy at midnight and alcohol leaves the body at the rate of a half-pint of beer per hour, so if Mary had died at 3.30am then there should have still been a quantity of it in her stomach. Not, however, if she had died much later. According to Caroline Maxwell, she vomited up her early morning drink. After that ginger beer, a tipple of hers, would have been good for an upset stomach but she may have had a little more alcohol consumed slowly so as not to vomit again, and as 'Clinical Forensic Medicine' points out, alcohol consumed in this fashion leaves the body as quickly as it enters it.

When we add all these factors together, ie: Bond's assessment being provably wrong, modern day comparisons and knowledge, the lack of alcohol and the fact that Mary was seen four or five times between 8.00 and 10.00am, then we can establish that the likeliest time of Mary Kelly's death was around 10.00am.

2000
THE LUSK KIDNEY REVISITED

CHRISTOPHER-MICHAEL DIGRAZIA

This is a revised and expanded version of the article 'Another Look at the Lusk Kidney' which appeared in Ripper Notes, Vol. 1. No. 4, March 2000, and was published in issue 29 of Ripperologist in June 2000

With, perhaps, the exception of the enigmatic Goulston Street Graffito, no object associated with the Whitechapel Murders has been the catalyst for more myth-making than the gruesome piece of extracted viscera known to posterity as the Lusk Kidney. Whether considered for the ghastliness of its presumed origin or merely for the questions inherent in its authenticity or falsity, few other artefacts connected with Jack the Ripper incite more dispute; few provide such an arena for opposing points of view, each side armed with seemingly incontrovertible evidence. The basic facts surrounding the kidney's arrival and identification are well known, but in light of the following discussion, they bear a brief recapitulation.

At about 5.00pm on Tuesday, 16 October 1888, a package was delivered to the home of George Akin Lusk, a builder living at 1 Alderney Road, Mile End. Since his appointment as head of the Whitechapel Vigilance Committee, Lusk had been the target for suspicious visitors and crank letters and at first sight the small, paper- wrapped cardboard box appeared to be one more such time-waster. However, after opening the parcel, Lusk was nonplussed to discover a small piece of rancid flesh enclosed with the following note:

> *From hell*
>
> Mr Lusk
>   Sor
>   I send you half the Kidne I took from one women prasarved it for you tother piece I fried and ate it was very nise I may send you the bloody knif that took it out if you only wate a whil longer
>   Signed   Catch me when you can
>   Mishter Lusk

Lusk's immediate reaction was that this was another in the series of eccentric communications and he was prepared to dismiss the offal as an animal's kidney. Reflecting further, however - and in light of the somewhat sinister tone of an earlier postcard he had received noting "you seem rare frightened" – he decided to mention the package at the next Vigilance Committee meeting. And so, on Thursday morning the 18th, committee treasurer Joseph Aarons, secretary Harris and members Reeves and Lawton arrived at Lusk's home to see the curious postal delivery for themselves. What happened next can best be told by an excerpt from the *Star* of 19 October:

> *As no definite conclusion could be arrived at, it was decided to call upon Dr. Wiles of 56 Mile End Road. In his absence, Mr. F. S. Reed, his assistant, examined the contents of the box and expressed the opinion that the article formed half a human kidney which had been divided longitudinally. He thought it best, however, to submit the kidney to Dr. Openshaw, the pathological curator of the London Hospital, and this was at once done. By the use of the microscope Dr. Openshaw was able to determine that the kidney had been taken from a full-grown human being and that the portion before him was PART OF THE LEFT KIDNEY. Immediately it occurred to the Vigilance Committee that at the inquest on the body of the woman Eddowes who was murdered at Mitre Square Aldgate, it was stated that the left kidney was missing, and in view of this circumstance, it was deemed advisable to at once communicate with the police. Accordingly, the parcel and the accompanying letter were at once taken to Leman Street police station and the matter placed in the hands of inspector Abberline. Subsequently the City police were*

The Lusk Kidney Revisited

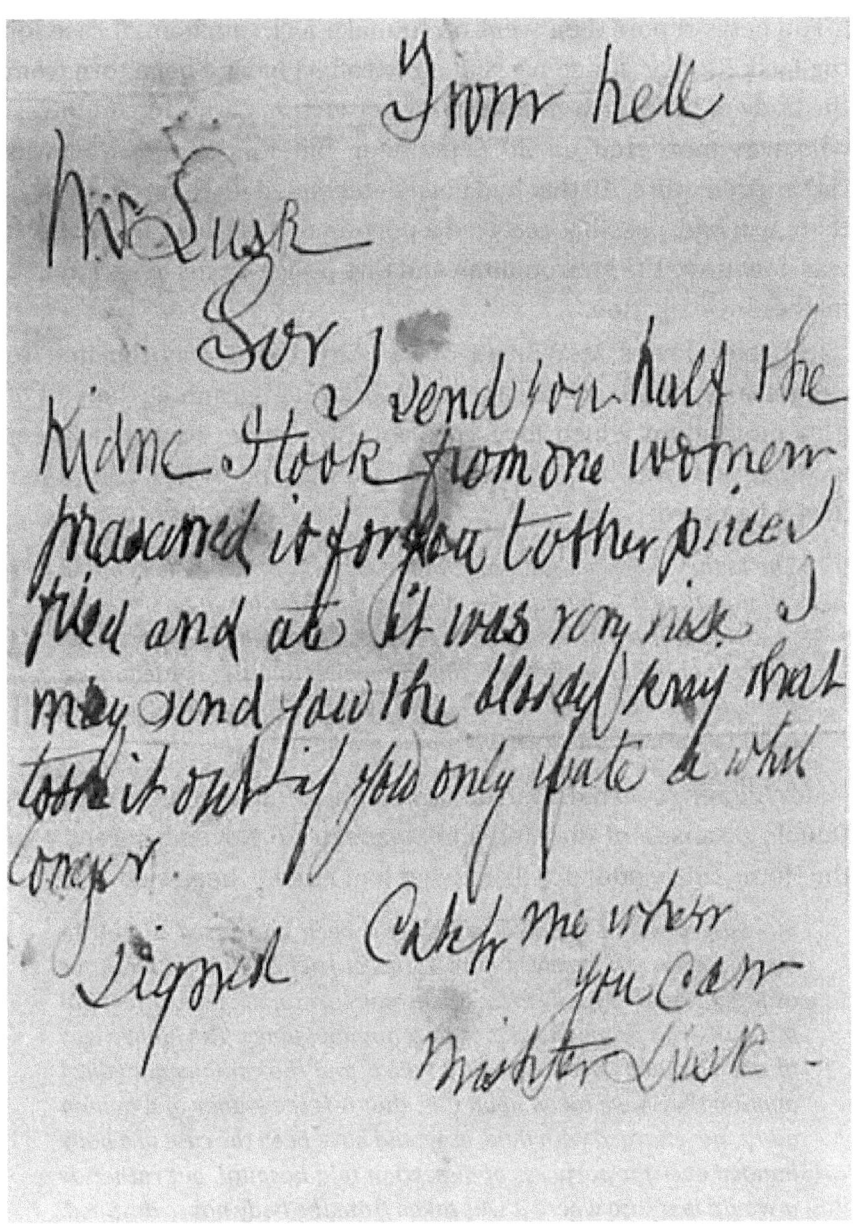

The letter sent to George Lusk, accompanied by a kidney

communicated with, as the discovery relates to a crime occurring within their jurisdiction.

The news report then went on to make a circumstantial case for the Lusk Kidney (for so we shall now call it) having been torn from the body of the fourth canonical Ripper victim, Catherine Eddowes, who was murdered on 30 September, but this supposition was rather premature. All that had been determined up to this point was that Lusk had, possibly, received a portion of a left human kidney. It was now up to the Metropolitan and City police forces to carry out a further investigation.

Inspector James McWilliam of the City Police was the first to submit a report on 27 October. In a brief paragraph at the end of a memorandum which focused primarily on the Goulston Street writing, Eddowes' inquest and the last sighting of her before her death, he noted:

The kidney has been examined by Dr. Gordon Brown who is of the opinion that it is human. Every effort is being made to trace the sender, but it is not desirable that publicity should be given to the doctor's opinion, or the steps that are being taken in consequence. It might turn out after all to be the act of a Medical Student who would have no difficulty in obtaining the object in question.

McWilliam reported that he "[met] daily" with Chief Inspector Donald Swanson of the Met, and Swanson's 6 November report to the Home Office added little to what had already been said:

*Mr. Lusk brought a parcel which had been addressed to him to Leman Street. He received it on 15th Oct [sic] and submitted it for examination eventually to Dr. Openshaw curator of London Hospital Museum who pronounced it to be a human kidney. The kidney was at once handed over to the City Police, and the combined medical opinion they have taken upon it is, that it is the kidney of a human adult; not charged with fluid, as would have been the case in a body handed over for purposes of dissection to a hospital, but rather as it would in a case where it was taken from the body not so destined. In other words, similar kidneys might + could be obtained from any dead person **upon whom** a post mortem had been made from any cause by students or dissecting room porter. [emphasis in original]*

All of this would seem to lead to the conclusion that the Lusk Kidney was a nasty joke; and, indeed, this appeared to be the police position by the beginning of November. However, as in so much else respecting Jack the Ripper, the newspapers defied such a simple answer and in the process raised questions which have bedeviled researchers and readers to the present day.

We need not quote from every press mention of the Lusk Kidney in our attempt to pronounce on its *bona fides*; only from those most often referenced in books on the Whitechapel murders and which have led to confusion over its authenticity. *The Star*, as we have seen, reported Mr. Reed and Dr. Thomas Openshaw as opining the flesh to have been half of a left human kidney. The Press Association, however - a news-gathering and disseminating organ similar to the infamous Central News Agency - supplied the *Eastern Post and City Chronicle* of 20 October with a much more lavish account. There, Openshaw was reported to have identified the Lusk Kidney as a "ginny kidney" - that is, one coming from someone who had been a heavy drinker, as well as being from a woman approximately 45-years-old. Furthermore, the report went on, the kidney had been extracted within the past three weeks, which, it was inferred, placed its removal within the timeframe of Eddowes' murder.

So far as we can determine however, Openshaw never expressed himself so freely on the subject of the Lusk Kidney. In both the *Star* and the *Telegraph* of 20 October, he merely held to the opinion that the kidney was human and that it *may* have been a left kidney. Certainly he was never again quoted so elaborately as in the Press Association report, and one is tempted to assign it to the fiction desk.

The solution to this quandary may lie in the *Telegraph* of 19 October. Within a story headlined "Mitre-Square Murder, An Extraordinary Parcel," Vigilance Committee treasurer Aarons was quoted relating his version of the events surrounding the kidney's identification. While the *Star* report earlier referenced implied that the entire party of committeemen went to see Openshaw, Aarons' *Telegraph* interview is revealing:

> *Mr. Reed... gave an opinion that it was a portion of a human kidney, which had been presented in spirits of wine; but to make sure, he would go over to the London Hospital...[o]n his return* **Mr. Reed said that Dr. Openshaw said** *that the kidney belonged to a female, that it was part of the left kidney, and that the woman had been in the habit of drinking. He should think that the person had died about the same time that the Mitre-square murder was committed.* [emphasis added]

An extraordinary identification, to be sure. But is there any truth in it?

Unfortunately, the answer must be 'no'. N.P. Warren, editor of *Ripperana* and himself a practicing surgeon, pointed out in 1989 the inherent absurdities of the above report. Even were Openshaw's supposed comments actually uttered by him, he could not have been absolutely sure of the sex of the Lusk Kidney, nor when its owner had died. As far as "the habit of drinking,", while Openshaw could have deduced Eddowes' tippling habits from the organ presented to him, alcohol damage to the human kidney comes as a result of years of chronic alcohol consumption, causing cirrhosis of the liver and subsequent hepatorenal failure.

So who is responsible for this imaginative set of findings which have influenced almost all later theorists? If Openshaw was not backtracking from a hasty and quickly public diagnosis, then we are left with Reed, Aarons or the Press Association. From the wording of the *Telegraph* article, the finger of guilt wavers between Reed and Openshaw, but at this remove it is impossible to tell. We can only put the 19 October story aside, as it contains nothing to prove the Lusk kidney's authenticity.

The same may be said of yet another series of comments on the kidney, these found in the 1910 memoirs of former City Police Commissioner Major Sir Henry Smith. Within the pages of his From Constable to Commissioner, he sets out to finish the matter of the Lusk Kidney once and for all:

> *I made over the kidney to the police surgeon, instructing him to consult with the most eminent men in the profession, and to send me*

> *a report without delay. I give the substance of it. The renal artery is about three inches long. Two inches remained in the corpse, one inch was attached to the kidney. The kidney left in the corpse was in an advanced state of Bright's Disease; the kidney sent me was in an exactly similar state. But what was of far more importance, Mr. Sutton, one of the senior surgeons at the London Hospital, whom Gordon Brown asked to meet him and another surgeon in consultation, and who was one of the greatest authorities living on the kidney and its diseases, said he would pledge his reputation that the kidney submitted to them had been put in spirits within a few hours of its removal from the body, thus effectually disposing of all hoaxes in connection with it.*

As with Openshaw's supposed findings, this is a stunning paragraph which would seem to put the provenance of the Lusk Kidney beyond question, and Smith's discourse constitutes one of the chief arguments in favour of it. It is important, therefore, that we examine his assertions carefully.

Sadly, Smith does not enjoy an unblemished reputation for veracity. He was known to his contemporaries as a charming raconteur, but one who tended to play somewhat fast and loose with the truth for dramatic effect. Several stories in his memoirs are palpably untrue, and his claim there to have once been 'five minutes' behind the Ripper is regarded as complete eyewash. While this less than complete dependability should not immediately prejudice us against Smith's account of the kidney, it is a caveat that must be borne in mind.

Let us begin then with the matter of the renal artery. The left renal artery is, indeed, generally 2-3 inches long. Beyond this, however, we cannot go. Smith is our only source for the comparative lengths of renal artery in, respectively, the Lusk Kidney and Eddowes' body. Dr. Frederick Gordon Brown, who conducted Eddowes' post-mortem and testified at her inquest, contented himself with remarking only that "the left renal artery was cut through." It is true that the *Telegraph* of 20 October stated

> *...it is asserted that only a small portion of renal artery adheres to the kidney, while in the case Mitre-square victim, a large portion of*

this artery adhered to the body,"

but Brown himself, when interviewed by *The Star of the East* on 22 October noted

> *as has been stated, there is no portion of renal artery adhering to [the kidney], it having been trimmed up. So consequently, there could be no correspondence established between the portion of the body from which it was cut.*

Taking into consideration Brown's familiarity with Eddowes' body as well as his denial of any renal artery remaining with the Lusk Kidney, in contrast to an anonymous press report and the anecdotal statement of Smith, the weight of evidence would appear to be against the famous 'one inch' of renal artery.

What, then, of the Bright's disease which we are told infected both the Lusk Kidney and Eddowes' remaining right kidney? The condition of 'Bright's Disease' takes its name from Richard Bright, an English internist and pathologist who first described the symptoms of this ailment in 1827. Today it is more commonly and specifically called 'chronic glomerulonephritis.' In 1888, however, the term was a catchall applied to a collection of signs and symptoms of kidney disease emanating from a variety of different causes - one of which was thought to be the excessive intake of alcohol. It should also be noted for the purposes of our discussion that in 1888 the term 'Bright's Disease' was also used as a synonym for 'nephritis', which is a non-suppurative inflammation of the kidney. This ailment was not uncommon among the poor and destitute of the East End, and it would not be at all surprising were Catherine Eddowes to have suffered such a condition.

Dr. Brown's postmortem states that he found Eddowes' "right kidney pale, bloodless with slight congestion of the base of the pyramids," and N.P. Warren has noted that such a description clearly indicates Bright's disease. But again, we must remember that in the late Victorian era, almost every chronic kidney disease was lumped under poor Dr. Bright's name. We cannot currently take it as a given that Eddowes had this malady. Of course, even if it were proven beyond doubt that she did, this does not allow us to infer the existence of such disease in the Lusk Kidney.

We are once again confronted with a statement made only by Major Smith. He does not tell us who prepared the report presented to him which indicated bilateral Bright's disease (though the term "the police surgeon" may be an oblique reference to Gordon Brown), and the surviving descriptions of the Lusk Kidney provide us only with the frustratingly vague nomenclature of "distinct marks of disease" and "ginny kidney." Brown's previously quoted 22 October interview is of no help here; he only notes in passing that the kidney showed "no trace of decomposition." The most likely version of Openshaw's comments also made no mention of disease; in fact, the only references to a disorder in the Lusk Kidney are in the 19 October *Telegraph* and in Smith's memoirs, neither of which can be regarded as entirely trustworthy.

The Lusk Kidney may have shown signs of disease. If it came from a recent Whitechapel decedent, then such is entirely possible. However, based on the sketchy surviving evidence, we cannot say what that disease may have been and are not justified in assuming it to have been Bright's disease beyond a factor of relative probability.

And what of Mr. Sutton, pledging his reputation that the kidney had been placed in spirits within hours of its removal from Eddowes' tortured remains? Dr. Henry Gawen Sutton was a senior surgeon and lecturer in pathologic anatomy at the London Hospital in 1888. He is not, however, mentioned in any of the surviving contemporary accounts of the investigation of the Lusk Kidney. Neither in any writings or remarks by Brown – who supposedly asked to meet him in consultation - not by Swanson or McWilliams, nor even by the gentlemen of the press. We find Sutton and his confident opinion *only* in the pages of Smith's memoirs. If he truly made any report on the kidney, it has not yet been found. Perhaps there was such a report; perhaps, too, his participation was a bit of dramatic license on Smith's part. We do not know. We will not know unless independent proof of Sutton's pronouncements turns up, and until then both he and Smith must be set aside.

We have now examined contemporary and near-contemporary sources concerning the Lusk Kidney. At this point, what can we say about its origin? In forming an opinion, we must consider both the descriptive and medical evidence. We can do no better in marshalling our arguments than by revisiting the seven points of identification proposed by N.P. Warren in his 1989 *Criminologist* article, "A Postal Kidney":

> The Lusk Kidney was human;
> It came from a woman;
> It came from a person approximately 45 years old;
> It had been extracted from the body within three weeks of its examination;
> It came from an alcoholic;
> It was severely affected by Bright's disease;
> It had approximately 1 inch of renal artery adhering to it.

The Lusk kidney was human

This would appear to be beyond reasonable doubt. Were the kidney to be presented to a modern pathologist, he would determine its origin either through karyotyping (by looking at the chromosomes) or genotyping (looking at the genes within the chromosomes). In 1888 however, neither type of analysis was available, and examination of the kidney to determine its human origin was through visual and morphological means, i.e., through the form and structure of the organ.

No medical man who examined the kidney considered it to be anything but human. The only dissenting opinion came from Dr. William Sedgwick Saunders, the Medical Officer and Public Analyst for the City of London, in the *Liverpool Daily Post* of 20 October, where he was quoted as saying:

> It is a pity some people have not got the courage to say they don't know. You may take it that there is no difference whatever between the male and female kidney. As for those in animals, they are similar, the cortical substance is the same, and the structure only differs in shape. I think it would be quite possible to mistake it for a pig's.

We must bear in mind, however, that Saunders was, in this instance, responding to a reporter who had asked him to comment on an unknown "medical man's" report that the Lusk kidney was that of a woman. Saunders' brusque response - one can almost hear him snorting with impatience! - was in regard to the supposed declaration of the sex of the kidney, and his 'pig' remark appears to have been an added fillip. Saunders did make the legitimate point that a human and animal kidney might well have been confused, and this should be kept in mind. We know that both Openshaw and Brown were reported as coming to their determination that the Lusk Kidney was human after microscopic examination; we do not know what other evidence, if any, assisted their conclusion. We should, in this case, trust to their competence, assume Lusk was sent half a human kidney, and let this point stand.

It came from a woman

As with point 1, this would be impossible to tell in 1888 other than through gross morphology. In general, the female kidney is smaller and lighter than the male, but in the case of the Lusk Kidney, we must take into consideration that it was not a whole kidney and that it may have been constricted as a result of Bright's disease. These two factors make identification of sex extremely difficult. As we have seen, once the kidney was determined to be human, thought immediately turned to Eddowes' murder. We must consider the possibility that her death and the "From hell" letter influenced many of those who pondered over the kidney, presuming it to be female because the letter said that it was. The verdict on this point should be 'not proven.'

It came from a person approximately 45 years old

Even despite the great medical strides made in the 20th century, a modern doctor would no more be able to answer this question than could his Victorian colleague. N.P. Warren points out that a rough guess as to age might be possible based on the condition of arteries remaining in the kidney, but such an absolute determination of age "is altogether too precise." He also notes that "a kidney may shrink by up to 1 cm in length between the ages of 30 and 70, [but] a Bright's kidney is pathologically constricted anyway." We must remember the temptation to immediately identify the Lusk Kidney with Eddowes' murder; combining such with the medical evidence, we can discard this point of identification.

It had been extracted from the body within three weeks of its examination

The Lusk Kidney was noted to have been 'preserved' in spirits of wine. Leaving aside the question of whether such an agent points to a freshly slaughtered body or one from the dissecting room, the mere mention of preservation speaks against such a precise determination of time. As well, we might also note that the initial mention of preservation comes from the already-suspect Aarons interview. Further to this point, we may look at Brown's previously quoted *Star of the East* statement, during which he informed the reporter that:

> As it exhibits no trace of decomposition, when we consider the length of time that has elapsed since the commission of the murder, we come to the conclusion that the possibility is slight of its being a portion of the murdered woman of Mitre Square.

This point of identification, while raising the intriguing possibility that the Ripper could have placed Eddowes' kidney into a vial of spirit immediately after her death, might best be discarded.

It came from an alcoholic

This point may be discarded as well. While alcohol can damage the kidney, this is a result of years of chronic drinking and even the preservation of half a kidney in spirits of wine would not contribute to a diagnosis of alcoholism. In 1888, medical opinion held that one of the causes of Bright's disease (which Eddowes may have had) was excessive alcohol intake – hence the lay term 'ginny kidney.' Thus, whatever medical condition was evidenced by the Lusk Kidney was taken as resultant from Eddowes' presumed dipsomaniacal habits and regarded as evidence of Bright's disease. It is worthwhile, however, to remember that no comprehensive medical description of the Lusk Kidney now exists. Gordon Brown's report on it has been lost, as has any report that may have been prepared by Sutton. We know only that it was a human kidney possibly preserved in spirits of wine; other reports of its pathological condition, as we have seen, come from unreliable sources.

It was severely affected by Bright's Disease

As has been noted, the reported condition of Eddowes' right kidney has led to the contested conclusion that she may have suffered from Bright's disease. However, in lieu of a comprehensive, contemporary medical description of the Lusk Kidney, we cannot yet presume that it, too, manifested such signs of disease. Our only source for this diagnosis is Major Smith. This point is not proven, but is possible.

It had approximately 1 inch of renal artery adhering to it

Our sources for this point of identification are Smith and the *Telegraph* of 20 October. Both appear to be trumped by Gordon Brown's statement that the Lusk Kidney had been 'trimmed up' and as he was in the midst of examining the organ when he said this, we might take his word as definitive. Yet perhaps the verdict on this point should be a very guarded 'possible,' bearing in mind that the Kidney had passed at the least from its sender (whomever he may have been) to Lusk to Reed to Openshaw to Abberline before being examined by Gordon Brown. It must remain as a possibility - though no more than a remote one - that the renal artery had been 'trimmed up' before Brown saw it.

At the end, then, a totaling of the seven points of identification leaves us with one positive, three negatives and three uncertains. Of the latter, two are no more than cautious probables and one most likely improbable. What then can we believe the best, though not yet final verdict?

After consideration of the extant medical and narrative statements, and bearing in mind that the current absence of physical matter will always compromise a dispassionate analysis of the case, it would seem to this author that the lack of evidence regarding sex, Bright's disease or renal artery concerning the Lusk Kidney assign it to being what the much put-upon George Lusk first thought it to be when it arrived at his door that late afternoon over one hundred years ago - a macabre practical joke, and no more.

Sources

Collection of Stewart P. Evans; *Star*, 19 October 1888; HO 144/221/A49301C.folios 169-170; HO 144/221/A49301C, folio 192; *Eastern Post and City Chronicle*, 20 October 1888; *Star*, 20 October 1888; *Daily Telegraph*, 20 October 1888; *Daily Telegraph*, 19 October 1888; N.P. Warren, "A Postal Kidney," T*he Criminologist*, Spring 1989. pp. 12-15; Sir Henry Smith, *From Constable to Commissioner*. Chatto & Windass. London, 1910, pp. 154-155; Inquest deposition of Dr. Brown, 4 October 1888. Corporation of London Public Records Office, ff. 14-21; *Star of the East*, 22 October 1888; Richard Whittington-Egan, *A Casebook on Jack the Ripper*. Wildy and Sons, London. 1975, pp. 59-60; *Liverpool Daily Post*, 20 October 1888.

The author wishes to thank Stewart P. Evans, Alex Chisholm, Thomas Ind, M.D. and Wayne Wivell, M.D., for their assistance and advice during the writing of this essay.

2001
ROBERT JAMES LEES: THE MYTH AND THE MAN

STEPHEN BUTT

This article appeared in edition 34 of Ripperologist

There is a general agreement amongst researchers that the alleged involvement of the medium Robert James Lees in the police investigation into the Whitechapel murders cannot be regarded as a factual account. Some would say that if Lees did have any association with the investigation, then the facts have been undermined by more fanciful narratives such as the *Chicago Sunday Times-Herald* article of 28 April 1895. Others simply believe Lees to have been a fantasist, and that the story developed from these fantasies with additional material, from his devoted daughter, Eva, and his spiritualist followers.

The story has survived largely because it has been an attractive subject for novelists, and for the makers of television programmes and films. Moreover, generations of spiritualists have accepted it almost as a tenet of their faith. Eva Lees played an important role in this, acting as her father's confidante and secretary, marketing her father's image as effectively as any modern media executive.

The credibility of the Lees story has been further eroded by misunderstandings that have crept into research. For instance, Nicholas P. Warren, in his article 'The Great Conspiracy' states:

> *The idea of a doctor was taken up by the maverick medium Robert James Lees (1849–1931) who just before his death claimed in the Daily Express to have solved the crime and received a royal pension for his pains.*

Lees died on Sunday 11 January 1931. The *Daily Express* articles, based on the earlier *Chicago Sunday Times-Herald* material, commenced almost two months after his death, on Saturday 7 March 1931. The claims in the *Daily Express* are not those of Lees. Nick Warren is actually referring to an *Illustrated Leicester Chronicle* feature which, as it happens, was written by a spiritualist. In other writings, the romantic but fictional presentation is of Lees as an old man with a long white beard, using a lifetime of psychic experience to stalk his prey. In fact, Lees was just thirty-nine years old in 1888, his 'career' as a medium was less than six-years-old, and he was an active family man with a wife and nine children aged between eighteen years and just eighteen months.

However, despite the doubtful provenance of many of the claims, it is certain that Lees did take an active interest in the murders. His diary for the first week of October 1888 records his attempts to work with the police:

> *Tuesday 2*
> *Offered services to the Police follow up East End Murders – called a fool and lunatic. Got trace of man from the spot in Berner Street.*
>
> *Wednesday 3*
> *Went to City Police again – called a madman and fool.*
>
> *Thursday 4*
> *Went to Scotland Yard – same result but promised to write me.*

It is also clear that his work as a journalist and philanthropist, did bring him close to the people affected by the Ripper's activities, as we shall see by considering Lees' life and career.

Robert James Lees was born on 12 August 1849 in the Leicestershire

Robert Lees circa 1898

market town of Hinckley. His father, William Lees, is listed in the trade directories as a grocer, baker, flower dealer, publican and shopkeeper. At the time, Hinckley's main industry of stocking hose manufacture was in decline and it is likely that William Lees suffered from the downturn in the economy, attempting to earn a living in any way possible. The family moved in September 1861 to Rugby and then to Birmingham, settling by 1867 in the Aston district. The move was probably in order to seek trade in a more prosperous area, but perhaps in order to escape from the debt. Legal papers indicate that William Lees was never successful as a businessman. He died a pauper in the Liverpool workhouse on 13 May 1880.

Lees married the daughter of an Aston silversmith, Sarah Ann Bishop, at the Erdington Congregational Chapel on 17 December 1871. Their first child, Norman, was born in the Birmingham area in 1873. Given that he was to become a journalist and writer, it is surprising to note that Lees had little formal education, as he was needed to assist in the family's businesses. However, his father turned to printing as a further means of earning a living, and Lees' occupation on his marriage record is given as a 'compositor'. This may have been the qualification that enabled him to obtain a post in the advertising section of the *Manchester Guardian* where he was working by 1876.

The newspaper sent Lees to London in 1878 to investigate establishing a bureau there. However, whilst in London, Lees was offered a post on one of the new journals being launched at that time, and chose to leave the security of the *Manchester Guardian*. The 1881 Census records that Lees' son Lionel was born in September 1877 in Lancashire, and his next surviving son, Bernard, in Surrey in December 1878. This census and references in *The Heretic*, his only autobiographical work, suggest that Lees' move to London took place early in 1878.

The Heretic tells of Lees' years in London. It tells how he fell victim to fraud and so lost his job, home and possessions. On New Year's Eve 1878, he contemplates committing suicide by jumping off London Bridge, but is rescued by kindly stranger who provides both moral and physical help. Subsequently, in the true manner of a Victorian melodrama, the criminals who forced such suffering on Lees are brought to justice.

For some time, Lees is dependent upon the generosity of friends, but his fortunes improve after chance meeting with American visitors near Westminster Abbey. This leads to a new occupation as a guide to visiting Americans. Eventually, he is able to return his family to the more affluent lifestyle. His work as a guide leads him to the poorer areas of London, and to establish an organisation offering people a means of maintaining their self-respect. This enterprise, the People's League was launched on 18 November 1893 in Peckham.

The Heretic was written to explain how the material crises of his years in London helped Lees to rediscover his earlier belief in spiritualism. He saw three separate eras in his life, namely his early psychic encounters which dated from his cradle days, the years of doubt after being deceived by two fraudulent mediums when he campaigned actively against spiritualism, and the period after his 'return' to spiritualism.

He was, without doubt, a gifted speaker and a skilled writer, but his personal theology and ideology separated him from both orthodox Christianity and organised spiritualism. As a Christian spiritualist, he was shunned by most Christian denominations, but he also refused to support the 'showier' aspects of spiritualism. After his return to spiritualism, he declined to affiliate himself to any particular spiritualist organisation. In his later years, he was much admired by spiritualists in general, and his books remained influential for several decades after his death, but his staunch, almost arrogant non-conformist critical style meant that he would never become popular leader.

Incidentally, Lees' description of his return to spiritualism, published in *Light*, the journal of the College of Psychic Studies, on 22 May 1886, was a source for the Chicago article of 1895. In *Light*, Lees describes debating his new theory about spiritualism with two acquaintances:

My theory... was immediately accepted by a Mr. S, a gentleman of some scientific standing, who was also a Spiritualist (and) another of the company, Mr. B, who wished to join us, the latter being an Atheist. An arrangement was made to sit a certain number of times, under conditions to which we all agreed... Let me here say both these gentlemen were Americans. In answer to further enquiries, Mr. B was told to reopen the workings of a certain mine... After a slight pause, an address was given... corresponding with eight p.m. English time... At my suggestion we arranged to sit that same night, and about twenty minutes past eight Mr. S was told his cable had been received...

In the Chicago article, this séance becomes an occasion when Lees foresees another Ripper murder, and the two American gentleman acquire names. The reference of the time is retained, but the actual time stated is changed:

Shortly after this Mr. Lees returned to England where he made the acquaintance of Roland B. Shaw, a mining stockbroker, of New York and Fred C. Beckwith, of Broadhead Wis, who was then the financial promoter of an American syndicate in London. These three gentlemen were dining one day in the Criterion when Mr. Lees turned to his and two companions suddenly and exclaimed: "Great God! Jack the Ripper has committed another murder". Mr. Shaw looked at his watch and found it was eleven minutes to eight. At ten minutes past eight a policeman discovered the body of a woman in Crown court...

If compared to the work of Barnardo and other philanthropists of the time, the People's League was a small operation. However, despite its small scale and its short life (it lasted for just seventeen months and closed in April 1895) it was certainly successful. Membership reached 1,600 by 1 January 1895, when the League gave a free New Year's Day Tea no less than 618 destitute children in one sitting.

The League was based on principle similar to those of the earlier friendly societies. It comprised several separate financial groups, each of thirty-three members. Each member contributed 6 pence (6d) per week, and each group was responsible for purchasing one commonly used commodity. The League was therefore able to purchase, for instance, several hundred tons of coal at trade price to be delivered to each member as required. The members therefore receive more cold than they would normally have been able to purchase individually from a merchant.

Sarah Lees ran a clothing department where she taught local women to make up garments for material purchased in a similar way. One of the aims was to provide a uniform and other clothing for girls seeking employment in domestic service. Girls were able to attend interviews dressed smartly, and when they had obtained a position, were kitted out with a pack of necessary garments. A girl could repay the League in instalments, when she received a regular wage, so the repayments could be used to fund future activities, and the League's work could be accepted by the proud poor as a 'helping hand' rather than as a charitable gift.

The closure of the People's League coincided with the publication of the Chicago article in the Spring of 1895. According to his diary, Lees was in St Ives in Cornwall, convalescing after a prolonged period of illness when the article was published:

> *I left London again on April 20th with Mrs. Lees and remained here until June 7th (seven weeks)...*

There are suggestions in the diary that other events during 1895 had been the cause of Lees' ill health, and had prompted the closure of the League and the move to the West Country. Spiritualists would argue that he was directed to do so, by his spirit guides or by Queen Victoria.

It is interesting to compare the change in the tone of Lees' diaries for 1895 and 1896. Looking back over the events of 1894, Lees' entry in the former diary abounds in positive memories:

> *It's not to pass away time, that goes all too swiftly as it is, but that I may jot down, if time will allow me, a few items of my work in this glorious league, that I open this book. A work that has grown so rapidly and is doing such mighty service should not have all record of its progress lost, and one great regret I have is that I did not attempt to write its career down from the foundation, but who*

thought it would assume such proportions?

In comparison, the corresponding page at the commencement of the following year's diary looks back on what had obviously been a very traumatic year:

> *What a lapse of time since I opened this book, and what a record in the interval. It has been too heartbreaking to wish to write it down. Officialdom, work, worry and other things have all combined to break down my health and destroy my glorious work. As usual I tried to do too much, the burden was heavy, the strain too great, and man's inhumanity to man too indescribable to be continued.*

Of course, this emotional outpouring demonstrates Lees' pompous view of his work, and shows that he had faced opposition during 1895, but there is no direct reference to the Chicago article. It is certainly possible that Lees was so ill when the article was published that he did not know of its existence or of the versions in British newspapers such as *The People* on 19 May 1895. Perhaps by the time he was well enough to respond, public interest had waned. From his own diary, it is possible to draw up the following schedule of Lees' movements at the time:

8 March 1895:
To Saint Ives. Stayed three weeks

29 March 1895:
To London. Stayed three weeks

20 April 1895:
To Saint Ives. Stayed 17 days

28 April 1895:
Chicago article published

19 May 1895:
The People article published

7 June 1895:
To London. Stayed five days

12 June 1895:
To Saint Ives. Settled permanently.

Eva Lees saw the move to Cornwall as a form of exile. It also marked the point where the narrative of *The Heretic* ends. On its final page, writing in third person, there is anger and disappointment in Lees' words:

> *For the third time (he) turned his face towards his… exile, this time carrying his family with him. The quiet of the long-wished-for days has come back again to Elinor (Sarah), but a black shadow of regret hangs over them…Day by day…he walks along the rugged coast listening to the ceaseless anthem of the Atlantic waves, speculating whether he will ever find such help as will enable him to return and go on with his regrettedly-interrupted labours. It is years since the doors of the brotherhood were closed but it will never be forgotten.*

Lees remained in St Ives for five years, occupied mainly in writing and in correspondence with other spiritualists. He preached from non-conformist pulpits in the town and clashed with the powerful Mayor of St Ives over the issue of temperance. His closest friends, it seems, were the pilchard fisherman who presented him with a silver loving cup when he moved on to Plymouth in 1900.

In the past, those critical of the Lees Ripper story have regarded it as his own account. However, there is very little evidence that Lees ever discussed the Whitechapel murders with anyone other than his closest friends or that, either at the time of the murders or in the period before the Chicago article, he made any public pronouncements on the subject. Even his own daughter, Eva, denied that her father had written an account of his alleged involvement. Despite the dramatic claims in the *Daily Express* and the *People*, following his death, Eva denied emphatically that any 'secret document' naming the identity of Jack the Ripper existed. In an interview for *Le Matin* published on 22 March 1931, she seemed to have attempted to set the record straight:

> *The information given recently to the public has not been given by me. It is from someone who knew my father and who received from him certain confidences, and who was thought well to act as he has done. He is a journalist, and I have not wished that he should do it.*

On being asked to produce the secret document that other

newspaper reports referred to, giving the identity of Jack the Ripper, Eva replied:

> *I should not be surprised that an original document exists, but I am not able to show it to you for the very simple reason that I have not yet had the time to look over all the papers that my father has left... If there is truly an account written by his own hand, I have not helped at its drawing up, and for the moment I am unaware even of its existence.*

Eva's brother, Claude, even wrote to the editor of the *Daily Express*, demanding to know the source of their articles. The newspaper refused to disclose any information. Apart from the Chicago article, the first published report associating Lees with the Jack the Ripper investigations appears to have been an *Illustrated Leicester Chronicle* article written on 23 November 1929 by Hugh Mogford.

Mogford had encountered Lees some years earlier in Ilfracombe when covering the story of Kathleen Thomas who was attempting the first Bristol channel endurance swim. Subsequently Mogford became a spiritualist and interviewed Lees in that capacity, rather than as an objective journalist. However, even Mogford declined to suggest that a secret document existed. If he knew of one, he would certainly have used it.

Spiritualists have always regarded Lees' alleged association with Queen Victoria as being of greater significance than the Jack the Ripper story. Understandably, if it was known the Queen Victoria believed in the spirit world, then the movement, beset with accusations of fakery and fraud, would have benefited greatly. Here again, no firm evidence exists support the claim that Lees, as a child medium, enabled the grieving Victoria to contact the spirit of the late Prince consort.

Elizabeth Longford, in her biography of Victoria is dismissive of the entire story, but bases her doubts on several curiously irrelevant matters including the confusing issue of the so-called 'royal' copy of Lees' first novel, *Through the Mists*, and also the problem of the 'royal envelopes'. Frequently, Eva Lees would show these items to enquirers as proof of her father's association with the Royal court.

The book is a copy of Lees' first work, bound in crimson morocco with the royal cipher stamped in gold on the front cover. Eva claimed that the book had been bound at the Queen's request and presented to Lees in gratitude for his help. Eva also owned four small envelopes, each bearing the royal cipher, which she claimed once held private letters from the Queen. These claims came to public knowledge mainly through the publication of *The Curse of Ignorance* by Arthur Findlay. In this book, Findlay recounts the story of Lees 'alleged association with Queen Victoria and states categorically that:

> *Queen Victoria ordered six specially bound copies (of Through the Mists) which she presented to members of her family.*

Findlay adds that:

> *The foregoing information was given to the author by his daughter Eva Lees, with permission to incorporate it in this book, and this is the first occasion that all the facts have been made public.*

In truth, the books were bound, not by Royal command, but at Lees' own request. The copy seen by Lady Longford was one of a number of copies similarly bound, four of which Lees subsequently sent to members of the Royal household. The four envelopes held nothing more than acknowledgements from the secretaries of the four royal recipients. The letters – or in fact cards – are still in existence, and reveal that the four recipients were the Duchess of York, Princess Henry of Battenberg, the Princess of Wales, and Queen Victoria herself.

Logically, whether the binding of these books was commissioned by Queen Victoria or by Lees, it neither confirms nor denies the authenticity of the basic story. Longford adds further doubt by stating that 'nothing of his royal connection... emerged until he died in 1931', when it is known that several leading journalists and spiritualists knew of Lees' claims as early as 1925. On 22 July 1925, an Isobelle H. McCall wrote to Lees, asking for details of the experiences he had as a medium for Queen Victoria. She felt that an explanation directly from him would further the cause of Spiritualism in Edinburgh. Lees replied on 2nd September, refusing to clarify his involvement, and asking Miss McCall to explain where she had heard it. His letter indicates that the general story had been in the public domain for some time:

> *If you wish me to confirm some report that has come to your knowledge as to what took place at those séances. Then I want to know what it is you have heard before I venture to admit or sanction the report in any way. I am compelled to do this because such wild and exaggerated statements have been made on this matter that I positively am unable to identify myself in connection with the affair, since what was originally no more than a more in the sunbeam, has now become a volcano of considerable proportions. This has become so annoying to me for some time past that I have been compelled not to reply to any enquiries concerning it, except to say that if, after I have finished my work and have passed to my rest, it should be thought necessary to publish, in any form, any account of the part I have been permitted to take in the evolution of Spiritualism, then the story as it really took place will be fully available, but in the meantime, I cannot undertake to do more than I have done to correct reports that are simply ridiculous. And I think you will agree with me.*
>
> *With all good wishes for your success in your endeavour,*
> *I am, in the Master's service,*
> *Very sincerely yours,*
> *Robert James Lees.*

On 10 November 1925, the journalist and spiritualist writer Hannen Swaffer wrote to Lees, asking if he could write up the story. Lees declined in a letter dated 12th November. In 1928, Sir Arthur Conan Doyle made a similar request, and again met with refusal. Conan Doyle's letter neatly sets out the basic story:

> *Dear Mr. Lees,*
> *I was wondering whether the remarkable story of the late Queen and your psychic experiences could not be put on record – even if it when not publicly used. It seems to me, so far as I understand it, to be a point of great historical interest.*
> *The general outline as it reached me was that as a young Medium you got a message from Prince A. That you sent it. That two Court Officials came to investigate. That they got messages. That these*

messages indicated JB as having the same powers as you, and that from then onwards JB did act is a medium.

We are all growing older and it would be good to leave a clear record behind.

Your sincerely,

A Conan Doyle

Melvin Harris, in *Jack the Ripper – the Bloody Truth*, argues that Lees could have easily responded publicly to the Chicago article, but did not do so because he realised the article was taking the rise out of him. Mr. Harris goes on to say that, after the *Leicester Chronicle* article of 23 November 1929, numerous journalists attempted to "wrest the name of the killer from Lees" and that 'fellow spiritualist Conan Doyle tried his best...but even he couldn't persuade Lees to divulge the name'. However, it is clear that Conan Doyle's motive for writing his 1925 letter to Lees was to gain credence for the Spiritualist movement by proving that the late Queen believed in spiritualism. That letter does not refer to Jack the Ripper. Moreover, it was written when Conan Doyle's spiritualist activities were being ridiculed, his reputation having been damaged by his support for fraudulent mediums and such incidents as the Cottingley Fairies. Harris does not reproduce Conan Doyle's letter nor does he give it provenance so it must be assumed that the above letter is not the one to which he refers.

Eva saw a clear link between her father's alleged séances with Queen Victoria and the Jack the Ripper affair. She claimed that Victoria later asked Lees to help track down the Whitechapel murderer, and that he received a royal pension that in part funded the People's League. Eva also said that the family's exodus to Cornwall in 1895 was at Victoria's behest. Possibly the only reference in Lees' writings that could support this is in his diary for that year:

Now I have had six months here, but I am scarcely able to say just where I stand. As a visitor I was welcomed and admired, as a resident, with my undoubted power of speech, and a financial position which no one knows anything about, I am regarded with very mixed feelings. I'm a very unknown quantity and that troubles everyone.

Regarding the lack of any firm evidence of Lees' contact with the spirit of Prince Albert, it must be stressed that at this time the British Spiritualist Movement was still in its infancy. Lees was born just one year after the Hydesville 'rappings' which had triggered the revival of spiritualism. If royal séances did take place, then they would have occurred around 1862 to 1864.

The first spiritualist newspaper, the *Yorkshire Spiritual Telegraph*, was not published until 1855, and no national organisation had been formed by then. If a description of the young Lees' experiences was published, it is likely to be in a local journal with limited readership and circulation.

Lees' involvement with American visitors to the capital, as a tourist guide and through his spiritualist contacts, provides a partial explanation for Eva's claims that her father knew of American-Fenian plots to terrorise London, and assisted the police in their investigations. There is also a suggestion in Eva's mind of an association between Lees and Sir Robert Anderson. In her mind at least, this provided a convenient connection between Lees and the police investigations into both the Fenian terrorist campaign and the Whitechapel murders.

As with so many of Eva's claims, the Fenian link is in easy target for Lees' detractors. This is a quite understandable response to the fact that Eva had a very convenient explanation as to why her father's name did not appear in any police, legal or court records, relating to Fenian trials. Quite simply, the police had all the evidence they needed without requiring Lees to give evidence.

Melvin Harris attributes the claim – that Lees was responsible for the capture in 1883 of the Fenian terrorist Thomas Gallagher and his accomplices – to Lees himself, and dismisses it. He says that the police were tipped off about Gallagher in Birmingham, not in London, and that they tracked down the gang's bomb-making factory there. Eva claimed that Lees was in the same London hotel as the gang when the police arrested them. Daniel Black, a friend of

Lees' family who wrote a brief biography of Lees in 1944, adds some further details:

> *Lee's was one day approached by five gentleman recommended by wealthy sugar broker in the USA who desired to have his services for several weeks with the object of being shown architectural points of beauty in all the leading public buildings. Time admitted, however only of six days being given. The first visit was to be to Westminster, the second to the Tower. Mr. Lees had a letter from Gladstone and the Earl of Shaftsbury giving him permission to enter any of the buildings under government control, also a letter from Lord Chelmsford, then keeper of the Tower. The five wanted Mr. Lees to spend each evening with them to answer one thousand and one questions, which request met with a refusal. A timely warning reached him from the other side, asking him to report to Scotland yard, where the officer in charge took him for a madman, as he could get messages 'from the air'.*
>
> *At the tower at Beefeater informed Mr. Lee's there was no-one present but an old woman interested in sketching; if she bothered them he was to get her ejected by policeman. The old woman followed them and was ultimately put out; on receiving a further warning Mr. Lee's went to Scotland Yard, where he reported to one of the chief officials, who advised him to return to the restaurant and except the invitation of the five to dinner, remaining until 8.45pm. The supposed old woman was none other than a detective from Scotland Yard. At 8.40pm Mr. Lees suggested they should go through and read the American news just coming in. Six 'Americans' entered at 8.45, then (an)other six, in search of a certain newspaper they finally came round to the table of Mr. Lees and found it there, but by that time there were actually two detectives standing behind each of the five tourists.*
>
> *"You are our prisoners," came the sudden and stern announcement. The trial of Dr. Gallacher and his four confederates (American Irish Fenians) terminated in a sentence of twenty years' hard labour – a long term sentence being passed on the others – for an attempt to blow up the Houses of Parliament. The Scotland Yard officials acting on information given by Mr. Lees had proceeded to the hotel of the five, and there found incriminating papers, thus rendering unnecessary any references being made to Mr. Lees in the criminal proceedings."*

Another letter exists that would add further support the claim that Lees was actively involved in passing on information about American Fenians to the authorities, albeit at a later date. This is the note signed "F. Powell" to Lees dated 20 August 1894:

> Sir,
> I have been directed by Mr. Anderson, Director of Criminal Investigation Dept Scotland Yard, to call you and thank you for your kind offer of assistance re anarchists and to say that he will avail of the offer to the fullest. With this object I am instructed to attend to the matter and would like to see previous to next meeting night or say at your house at 7pm subject of course to your own convenience. If you can make a more suitable arrangement if you would be good enough to drop me a line I will be delighted to attend to it.
> Yours etc,
> F. Powell.

The note does not seem to support the view that Lees was ignored by authorities, nor that he had no credibility with the police after he contacted them at the time of the Ripper murders. Although it could be argued that any offer of information about Fenian activity would be routinely followed up, the tone of this letter would suggest that this was not a routine reaction, but a serious response to the previous offer of information from Lees.

In 1900, Lees moved with his family from St Ives to Plymouth, and less than two years later he moved again, to Ilfracombe in Somerset. Then began a quarter of a century of reclusive retirement, when Lees wrote further novels about the afterlife, and continued an active correspondence with spiritualists throughout the world. His wife Sarah died in 1912, and eventually his many children left home, some moving as far away as America and Australia. Only Eva remained with him.

In 1928, they moved back to Leicestershire. After several years of poor health, Lees died at his home in Fosse Road, Leicester on 11 January 1931. He was cremated at the city's Gilroes Crematorium, and his ashes were returned to Ilfracombe to be interred in his wife's grave. The brief interment service, attended by a few family friends, ended a life of drama but marked the beginning of an era of debate and controversy regarding this unusual man.

Addendum

Since this article was first published, research has established a connection between the authors of the *Chicago Sunday Times-Herald article* and the Lees family. It was already known that the newspaper editor and spiritualist W.T. Stead visited Chicago shortly before the article was published. Letters written by Stead confirm that Lees' sons Norman and Lionel were also living in Chicago at that time. In one letter, Stead describes Norman as 'the young English police reporter'.

Norman, the eldest of Lees' children, was eleven years old at the time of the Whitechapel Murders. He eschewed his parents' beliefs in spiritualism, and claimed that news that he had secured a job in Chicago was conveyed to his parents in England by spirit guides. Arguably, Norman had an even more eventful life than his father. He was for some time imprisoned in the Mattawean State Institute, New York State, for allegedly setting fire to his house, and then emigrated to Australia where in 1916 he enlisted in the Australian Imperial Force and served in a trench mortar battery.

He died at a Salvation Army hostel in Sydney in 1942. His death certificate noted 'no known relatives' although several of his children and his siblings were alive in England and America.

Roland Shaw and Frederick Beckwith, referred to in the Chicago newspaper article have also both been identified.

References

London: *The Daily Express*, 'How I Caught Jack the Ripper!", March 7th 1931 p.7; 'Clairvoyant Who Tracked Jack the Ripper' March 9th 1931 p.3; 'Jack the Ripper's End', March 10th 1931 p.3. These are three articles reworked from the *Chicago Sunday Times-Herald* 1895 article.

The People (London) 'A Startling Story' by Joseph Hatton, 19 May 1895.

Paris: *Le Matin*, No. 124 de l'asile d'Islington 22 March 1931 p.1 and 29 March 1931 p.1 written by Bernarde Laporte.

Leicester: *The Illustrated Leicester Chronicle,* 23 November 1929 and 28 November 1929 written by Hugh Mogford.

'The Capture of Jack the Ripper', *Chicago Sunday Times-Herald*, April 28th 1895 p.23; reprinted in full in Melvin Harris: *Jack the Ripper - The Bloody Truth*, London: Robinson, 1999.

Light, the Journal of the College of Psychic Studies (London) 'The Rev. T. Ashcroft and Spiritualism', 15 May 1886 p.226 and 22 May 1886 p.241.

The Heretic, Robert James Lees, London: John Long 1901.

Manuscript sources

The following documents are in the Record Office for Leicestershire, Leicester and Rutland (ROLLR) catalogued under collection DE4481:

Robert James Lees. His diaries for 1894 and 1895/6. DE4481/214 and DE4481/215.

Letters of acknowledgement from members of the Royal family, January 1899. DE4481/1-1.

Letter from Sir Arthur Conan Doyle, 6 November 1928. DE4481/6

Letters from Isobelle H. McCall, 22 July 1925. DE4481/154 and 26 August 1925. DE4481/155.

Letter from Lees to Isobelle H. McCall, 3 September 1925. DE4481/156.

Letter from Hannen Swaffer, 10 November 1925. DE5581/157.

Letter from Lees to Hannen Swaffer, 12 November 1925. DE4481/158.

Black, Daniel, *A Biography of Robert James Lees* (unpublished), (Greenock, Scotland) 1940. DE4481/306.

Manuscript sources in private hands

Letter from F. Powell, 28 August 1894.

Letter from Claude Lees to the *Daily Express*, 1931.

Letter from the editor of the *Daily Express* to Claude Lees, 1931.

Lees' diary for 1888 is in the collection of the Spiritualist National Union headquarters at Stanstead Hall, Essex.

2002

MARY KELLY IS DEAD

JOHN MALCOLM

This article appeared in edition number 41 of Ripperologist

MARY KELLY IS DEAD.
AT LEAST WE CAN AGREE ON SOMETHING, OR CAN WE?

Many opinions are woven together with facts in order to rationalise the horrific crimes that occurred in London's East End near the end of the nineteenth century; many scenarios have been proposed, some easily embraced, others easily dismissed. The parameters are set by popular consensus, which is, again, formed by the combination of facts and opinion, for the indeterminate facts leave gaping holes in this ugly and sad story.

As tedious as this may seem, a re-examination of the basics should be a perpetual element, hand-in hand with speculation and the evaluation of new information. At times we move beyond the difficult questions and hope that leaping over these will land us the big prize. It's frustrating and nerve-wracking for those who have had more than just a casual interest in these crimes and times, but we persist in increasing numbers and with increasing vigor.

Of course the multitude of problems that one must deal with in a case such as this must begin with the distance of over a hundred years that separates us from the world of 1888 exponentially.

Now, with the advent of many sophisticated detection techniques and the birth of forensic science, criminal profiling, etc., we feel much more prepared and confident when approaching an unsolved crime, and this confidence is basically justified. This is true when it comes to modern crimes, but the further we go back in history, the more vague the details become, and this is why we should approach a mystery such as the Whitechapel murders with a certain degree of caution. It is much too easy to look back at the people involved and think them ignorant and uninformed in relation to our present day technology, but in turn we should be inclined to believe *ourselves* to be ignorant and at least under informed regarding the everyday ways of life and also the actual degrees of competence of the authorities in those times, relative to those times.

For instance, the criminal element has evolved parallel to those responsible for their detection; it is doubtful that the percentage of unsolved crimes is much different today than it was in 1888. Advances in the sciences of transportation etc. and the cultivation of the criminal mind over time have made it more difficult in many instances, the problems and solutions of detection increasingly more complex.

With that said, I would like to move on to examining several areas of debate, such as the relevance of the pre-canonical five victims, the focus on the 'Polish Jew', Sir Robert Anderson's words, weapons and 'anatomical knowledge', in which we've tended to use a 'this side or that side of the fence' approach generally as a means to solutions that ultimately fit our opinions, possibly to the detriment to our ultimate pursuit, which is, of course, to put a name and/or a face to Jack the Ripper.

Before I begin, I am inclined to start out on the defensive. I do not subscribe to any particular theory, nor do I feel close to formulating one of my own. There are certain opinions that I carry that tend to hold sway on my observations, but I continue to try to overcome these, for speculation is too easily transformed into fantasy. I really do feel that I would sleep better at night if this mystery were to be solved, and it would be a tremendous boost to my ego if I was to be part of that, but... I have no such expectations.

Mary Kelly is Dead

Sir Robert Anderson

That said, one of the many things that trouble me regarding contemporary research is how easily Martha Tabram and Emma Smith are excluded from consideration as far as being possible victims of 'you know who.'

Although obvious discrepancies in M.O. make it easy to dismiss these two (especially Smith), there are many common denominators that should complicate matters. The Canonical Five were all killed within a small area of the East End, lodged in an even tighter area, were in their forties (with the exception of Mary Kelly), were attacked on weekends or bank holidays and were, at least suspected of being involved in prostitution.

Smith and Tabram lodged in George Streeet (Nos. 18 & 19, respectively), which ran through Thrawl Street (Nichols, Kelly) into Flower and Dean Street (Nichols, Stride, Eddowes); Smith was approximately 45 and Tabram 39, both assumed to be of the same 'class'. Emma Smith was attacked at the corner of Osborn Street and Wentworth Street, Martha Tabram in George Yard, both locations almost directly in the centre of the other murder sites and within yards of each other.

Smith, by her account, was attacked by three men who had followed her from Whitechapel Church, presumably from her 'soliciting in and around Whitechapel High Street' which becomes Whitechapel Road at Osborn Street, which becomes Brick Lane at Wentworth Street. Mary Ann Nichols was seen walking alone in the Whitechapel Road at 11:30pm on her last night and again leaving the Frying Pan (on the corner of Thrawl Street and Brick Lane) at 12:30am. Police and the press made the connections of these first three of the Whitechapel Murders and only the subsequent murders, which had more in common with the murder of Polly Nichols, put any distance between hers and the earlier murders.

In all probability, the Whitechapel murderer did not begin his life of crime with the slaying of Polly Nichols. Without speculating on initial motives, the attack on Tabram may have been his first with a knife, which would explain the apparent sloppiness and subsequent refining of technique in the later killings. Now, as far as Emma Smith goes, even if she was assaulted by three men, who's to say that one of them couldn't have evolved into Jack the Ripper?

Clearly there was something uncommon about this particular crime (as suggested by press links to the later murders). We continuously hear of how brutal this area was at the time, but so far I have yet to see any examples of crimes that can be compared with even this one. The debate over the credibility and effectiveness of the FBI's criminal profiling program will be saved for another day, but the results of an interesting survey can be found in a book by Eric W. Hickey titled *Serial Murderers and Their Victims*:

> *Special agents from the FBI examined a sample of 36 sexual murderers, 29 of whom were convicted of killing several victims. Specifically, they were interested in the general characteristics of sexual murders across the United States. They explored the dynamics of offenders' sexual fantasies, sadistic behaviors, and rape and mutilation murders. These investigators noted several deviant sexual behaviors practiced before, during or after the victim has been killed. The act of rape, whether it be the actual physical act or a symbolic rape in which an object is inserted into the vagina, was found to be common among serial killers in this study. For some offenders, the act of rape served as only one form of sexual assault; they engaged in a variety of mutilations, sexual perversions, and desecrations of the victim's corpse (Ressler et al., 1988 pp. 33-44).*

As we know, Emma Smith's death was attributed to the effects of injuries caused by being raped with a 'blunt instrument.' This murder would appear to incorporate quite a few elements in the different cases of the Whitechapel murders, although again more points subject to debate. As for the robbery motive in the Emma Smith case, it seems as though each subsequent victim may have been robbed, considering that none of the victims were found to have any money whatsoever on their person when they were discovered - unless you are inclined to believe that, coincidentally, each victim was the first customer in each case. As for the murder of Martha Tabram, we generally tend to implicate her 'soldier client', when connecting Dr. Killeen's assessment of the wounds when referring to the single wound on the chest that could have been caused by a 'dagger or sword bayonet.' We know that, with the exception of that particular wound on the sternum, the others could have been caused by an 'ordinary penknife'. I am presuming this wound must have been caused by a 'strong' knife - one that could have withstood conflict with bone. What is unclear is whether or not the other wounds could have been caused by an instrument so described.

Another example of the use of statements from medical men to substantiate theories can be observed within the statements of Dr. Bagster Phillips when discussing the murder of Elizabeth Stride - 'the knife was not sharp-pointed; but round and an inch across. There was nothing in the cut to show the incision of the point of any weapon.' Now, from a knife being pulled across the throat, I don't quite understand how it could be ascertained that this was not necessarily 'sharp pointed,' especially if there was 'nothing in the cut to show an incision of the point of any weapon.'

Something that has not been discussed at length, or maybe not at all, could dispel a few particular doubts about whether different hands were responsible for slayings of Mary Kelly and Catherine Eddowes (which has been recently suggested, albeit to help fit a particular current theory) and also shed a different light on the questions of anatomical knowledge and/or medical skill of the murderer.

Catherine Eddowes had her uterus and one kidney removed and taken away. According to Dr. Thomas Bond, in his report on Mary Kelly, the uterus and kidneys were found together *with one breast* under the head. This would suggest that the removal of the kidneys and uterus were potentially part of the same operation, hence the missing uterus and kidney of Eddowes. My opinion of this would lend a hand to the unskilled version of the killer, mainly because if there is a more bizarre, complex explanation, it would seem as though the organs in question were in close enough proximity to have been removed together in a similar way in each case, without any specific intention- that in regard to the fact that with Eddowes the organs were taken away, whereas with Kelly they were not. This would also draw the similarities between the two cases together enough to make it less likely that more than one person was involved directly with the murders.

When questioning whether or not the murderer was seeking certain organs, why was it not apparent in the case of Polly Nichols, widely and generally agreed to be the first in the series? With Mary Kelly the motive certainly wasn't seeking organs, if it was the uterus that was the organ sought as with Annie Chapman and Catherine Eddowes.

The killer may not even have known exactly what he had in his pocket until after it became public knowledge of what was missing from Chapman's body. When he killed Eddowes, he may have been trying to copy *himself*...

It has become very difficult to resist the temptation to be influenced by the unequivocal affirmations made by Sir Robert Anderson, or at least hard to doubt his convictions regarding an obviously real suspect. We still cannot determine for certain the identity of this suspect and it is therefore pointless to argue guilt or innocence. We have narrowed our focus, as the police of 1888 did, and nothing has come to light to undermine these directions. Armchair profilers and Ripperologists alike will jump and scream otherwise. But honest debate is welcome; and honest conclusions will prevail.... or maybe not. Anyway... some things to think about when it comes to the Polish Jew theories:

If we accept that Aaron was the Kosminski who was later suspected in the murders, it can be noted that his residence at the time he was put away, Sion Square, was in extremely close proximity to the residence of John Pizer in Mulberry Street. And this location is certainly 'in the very heart of the district' where the murders were committed. This does not prove that these two men knew each other, but as Pizer had lived there for many years it seems like a possibility that they could have been acquainted. This seems also to reinforce the views that the police may have been focused on this particular area, and if Kosminski was in fact a murderer then the detection capabilities of the authorities, whether it be a form of early profiling (as an undefined practice) must be re-evaluated.

The practical applications of the common sense-based profiling techniques would show that it may not be a modern invention. In trying not to speculate, all of these generally accepted 'facts' would be very circumstantial evidence if a theory were to evolve from this.

Sir Robert Anderson's strong and direct statements in his memoirs show, at very least, that the police were, in fact, concentrating on very specific areas and suspects. His belief in identity of the murderer can be debated, but as far as we know, nothing he has said has been contradicted by anyone involved in the investigation. Major Henry Smith's attacks on Anderson for his 'irresponsible anti-Semitism' (*The Jack the Ripper A-Z*), for example, carry no more weight against Anderson's claims than the Swanson Marginalia carry in their favour.

To open another can of worms, Martin Fido's suggestion that Nathan Kaminsky could have been a possible candidate for official suspicion (if he was David Cohen... or maybe even if he was not) is made that much more fascinating by the fact that his residence has been given as just across the Whitechapel Road, approximately the same distance from Kosminski as Pizer and still closer to the sites where Smith and Tabram were killed.

What if one of these men had something to do with the Whitechapel murders? What if none of these men had anything to do with the Whitechapel murders? What if any of them were part of the three who attacked Emma Smith? What if these men were the three who killed her? If we cannot attach conclusions definitively, it seems as if it would be in our best interest to keep an open mind when thinking about possible solutions to these century old problems.

As unlikely as some of these senarios may seem to be, are these suggestions any more ridiculous than some of the popular contemporary 'theories'? And then there are the cases of Francis Coles, Alice McKenzie et al...

And by the way, have you noticed that the tourists who flock to the Ripper tours are the same people who gathered and gawked at the murder scenes and the funerals in 1888? Fascinated, detached, absorbed and dumbfounded by these inhuman atrocities, the tragedy of it all has left a lasting impression...

2003
MY SEARCH FOR JACK THE RIPPER

COLIN WILSON

This article appeared in edition number 48 of Ripperologist

In a Vanishing London I pick up the Grim Trail of Murder

When I was eight, someone lent my father a great red-bound volume called *The Fifty Most Amazing Crimes of the Last 100 Years.* (I'm not sure why, for I've never caught my father reading a book.) I was strictly forbidden to read it, in case it gave me nightmares. So I seized on it every time I was left alone in the house, and read it from cover to cover. I have a copy of it beside me as I write. At the top of every article there is a sketch of the criminal. Landru looks villainous and intellectual; Smith, who drowned his wives in a bath, is an unattractive nondescript; Crippen looks pathetic and hunted. But there is no drawing of Jack the Ripper; instead there is only a large black question mark. The question mark started me on my search for Jack the Ripper. It is not logical, of course, but the mind of a child is romantic and not logical.

Fascination

Why should the Ripper be more fascinating than Landru, just because he was never caught? No one has ever yet discovered how Landru destroyed every trace of his victim's bodies; in its way, this mystery is far more interesting than the identity of Jack the Ripper.

And yet it is the Ripper who exercises a fascination beyond any other mass murderer. Most mass murderers are boring little men, like Christie and Haigh - shifty, weak, unimpressive. Many of them have long criminal records - petty theft, swindling, burglary, confidence trickery - like Heath, Kurten, Dr. Marcel Petiot. Murder has not yet produced its Caesar, its Napoleon. Murderers are a dull lot. Perhaps the Ripper was a sneak-thief with many prison sentences behind him; perhaps it was only Wormwood Scrubs and not death, that put an end to his amazing career. We shall never be certain. All that we do know is that at least five murders of unparalleled brutality were committed in the latter part of the year 1888. Four of them took place in the streets of Whitechapel at night: the victims were all prostitutes (although none of them were what we would call "professionals").

Panic

All London panicked. There were meetings in the streets: bands of citizens formed themselves in vigilantes to patrol Whitechapel at night; thousands of men were questioned and released; men carrying black bags were attacked by mobs; the commissioner of police resigned. And finally, after a lull of more than a month, the Ripper committed yet another crime, this time indoors. The pieces of the victim - a girl in her early twenties - were left spread around the room like bits of a jigsaw puzzle. The panic reached new proportions; there were so many blue uniforms in Whitechapel that the place resembled a police barracks. And then nothing more happened. The murders stopped. In the following year, 1889, there were two more murders of prostitutes in the Whitechapel area, but without the same appalling mutilations; we shall never know whether the same man was responsible for these.

Tough

When I came to London in 1951, Whitechapel exercised a deep and powerful fascination over me. But it was no longer the Whitechapel that Jack the Ripper had wandered around.

Whitechapel is still a tough district, but by no means as tough as in 1888.

Sailors from foreign ships crowded the streets; there were dozens of cheap doss houses where the lay-abouts could sleep for as little as four pence a night. And although many "respectable" married women lived in Whitechapel, a large proportion of the female population was made up of non-professional prostitutes. Women without men, women whose men had left them, or simply women whose men spent their wages on drink.

It was a Whitechapel whose narrow, cobbled alleys were lit by gas lamps that stuck out of the wall; a Whitechapel where human derelicts slept out on the pavements or in entries at night; where murder and robbery was so commonplace that the newspapers didn't even bother to report them. This is the reason that the first two crimes attributed to the Ripper were not mentioned in the newspapers until the inquests.

All this has changed. In 1888, after the Annie Chapman murder, Bernard Shaw wrote a letter to the Press in which he suggested that the murderer was a social reformer who wanted to draw attention to social conditions in the East End. He was probably wrong; but German high-explosives have done what Shaw failed to do, and changed the face of Whitechapel. When I first visited Whitechapel, bombs had left great empty spaces, and many of the houses were windowless and filled with rubble. (After dark, tramps slept on the floors of these ruins.) Huge blocks of council flats had sprung up in Hanbury Street, only a hundred yards from the spot where Annie Chapman was murdered in a yard behind a barber's shop. The council school at the end of Old Montague Street stood black and empty, with political slogans chalked on its walls. Now the school has disappeared: only the black walls of the playground are still standing. The Whitechapel of the Ripper is disappearing day by day. in five years, it will be non-existent.

The First?

Who was the first victim of the Ripper? It might have been Emma

Smith, of George Street, Spitalfields, who was stabbed to death in Osborn Street.

Osborn Street is a sinister little thoroughfare that runs between Old Montague Street and the Whitechapel Road. Emma Smith lived for 24 hours after the attack, and stated positively that she had been assaulted and robbed by four men, one of whom stabbed her with an iron spike in the abdomen. It was a brutal and stupid murder; its victim was a pathetic, drunken prostitute of 45, who never had more than a few shillings in her purse. She was staggering home drunk at four in the morning when the attack took place. (There were no licensing hours in those days, and many pubs stayed open all night.) An hour later, she was admitted to hospital, her head bruised, her right ear almost torn off. Her death was due to peritonitis. At the time of the murders, many journalists stated that this was the Ripper's first crime. It seems unlikely, but the murder is worth mentioning for the insight it gives into the Whitechapel of seventy years ago. A man or woman might be found like this almost any morning, robbed and battered; it was too commonplace to report in the daily press.

Stabbed

Many criminologists believe that the murder of Martha Turner was quite definitely the first Ripper crime. This took place on August bank holiday, 1888. Martha Turner was a prostitute who lived in George Yard Buildings, Commercial Street. In the early hours of the morning, she was found on one of the outside landings of the lodging house; the post mortem revealed that she had been stabbed thirty-nine times with some weapon, possibly a bayonet. George Yard Buildings have disappeared, too - so completely that I have never been able to locate them. But since most of the buildings on the right hand side of Commercial Street date back further than 1888, it seems possible that they are still standing. The coroner revealed that the wounds had been inflicted by a left-handed man. Martha Turner had been seen talking to a guardsman on the evening before the murder, and since the injuries resembled bayonet wounds, the police started to look for a left-handed soldier. All the guards in the

Tower of London were paraded, but no arrest was made. Within a few weeks, the murder had been forgotten. How could anyone have guessed that a super-criminal was starting on a series of the most sensational murders of all time?

Amazing - how luck never deserted this killer.

No one knows the precise location of George Yard Buildings where Martha Turner, the Ripper's first victim, was stabbed to death. But we know the district. If you take a tube to Aldgate East station on a Sunday morning, you will see Whitechapel looking something like the Whitechapel of 1888. Wander up Middlesex Street - known as "Petticoat Lane" and you will find it hard to breathe among the crowds jammed around the market stalls.

Still tough

To your right and left there are still cobbled streets that looked exactly the same when Jack the Ripper walked through them in the "Autumn of Terror" in 1888. Turn off to your right, and walk fifty yards, and you will find yourself in Commercial Street - the heart and jugular vein of Whitechapel. Late at night, the police still walk two abreast along these pavements. It is a tough district. And yet if you come here at five o'clock on a Sunday afternoon, the quiet will surprise you. The market has closed; the people of Whitechapel are indoors having their tea or sleeping off their lunch time beer. This is the Whitechapel that you would not have seen in 1888. To begin with, the pubs would still have been open. Drunks would have been snoring in the small alleyways off Hanbury Street. But you would have been sensible enough not to explore the narrow alleyways, for your chances of being coshed and robbed would be very high. Probably in no other place in England was so much of the total income of the inhabitants spent on beer or spirits. And those were the days when pubs were approximately five times as numerous as today. Alcohol was their best chance of forgetfulness, the best way to stop being aware of dirt and overcrowding and near starvation. This may be the reason that the sadist known as Jack the Ripper chose Whitechapel for his hunting ground. In a sink of human misery, the individual life does not count for much. And the sight of a body, prostrate in an alleyway, causes no alarm.

In the gutter

In fact, this is what happened in the case of Mary Ann Nichols, the Ripper's second victim.

In the early hours of the morning of 31 August 1888, a carter named William Cross was walking along Bucks Row, Whitechapel, on his way to work. Bucks Row is another street that has not altered since 1888, although its name has now been changed to Durward Street. On one side of the road are small houses, all absolutely uniform; on the other side are blocks of warehouses. Cross noticed something on the other side of the street - a bundle which he took to be a tarpaulin. Then he saw it was a woman apparently drunk. She was sprawled out at the entrance to a stable yard, with her head in the gutter.

Puzzled

Another man walked up as he stood there, looking down at her. The newcomer said: "Come on, let's get her on her feet." They bent down to turn her over, and Cross jumped back, exclaiming: "Blimey, she's bleeding!" The other man confirmed this, and commented: "She's not drunk. She's perishing well dead." The two men ran off to find a policeman. And while they were away the body was rediscovered by another policeman. Within a few minutes, four men stood around the body. It was about four o'clock in the morning.

Both the policemen were puzzled. They had beats that took them past where the body was lying, and both of them had been in the street, at either end of Bucks Row, in the past quarter of an hour. Neither had seen anyone. Someone summoned Doctor Ralph Llewellyn, who, felt the woman's pulse, commented that she had been dead about half an hour, and told the police to take her to the mortuary at Old Montague Street workhouse. The noise of the discussion attracted several people from the nearby houses. A Mrs.

Emma Green, whose bedroom was within yards of the spot where the body was found, remarked that "whoever had done it" must have been very quiet, since she had been lying awake for several hours, and had heard no sound.

In the morgue, a young policeman lifted the woman's clothes to gain some idea of the extent of her injuries. What he saw made him vomit. The woman's body had been ripped open from the throat to the stomach. The policeman rushed off to find Dr. Llewellyn, who had to give him first aid before he hurried to the morgue.

Solved

The first problem was that of identification. This was solved quickly: her name as Mary Nichols; she was 42 years of age, and known to her friends and acquaintances as Polly. She had been married to a printer's machinist and had borne him five children, but they had been separated for seven years; her love of the gin bottle and the slovenliness that resulted from it had made him leave her. But as he stood over her body in the mortuary, he was heard to say: "I forgive you for everything now that I see you like this." Since her marriage broke up, Polly Nichols had sunk steadily lower. She had lived with several men in quick succession, had taken a job as a servant but had to steal from her employers to get money for drink, and had then gone to live in Whitechapel.

For drink

Here she lived as a prostitute, sleeping in nightly doss houses where a bed could be had for four pence. The main necessity was drink; she would go with a man for the price of a glass of gin - a few pence. A few hours before her death, Polly Nichols had arrived at the doss house in Thrawl Street, completely drunk and without money. The lodging house keeper turned her away. She had told him: "Don't worry. I'll soon get the money. Look what a fine hat I've got." An hour later, an acquaintance saw her at the corner of Osborn Street where Emma Smith had met her death a few months earlier, attacked by a gang on Easter Monday. Asked by the acquaintance if she was having any luck, Polly replied that she wasn't, and staggered off up Osborn Street, singing cheerfully to herself. She probably then turned right into Old Montague Street, and wandered towards Vallance Road at the end. And somewhere along here, she met a man.

Not certain

It is still not certain how Jack the Ripper killed Polly Nichols with so little sound. A bruise on her face indicates that he clamped his hand over her mouth as he cut her throat. They were standing on the three- foot wide pavement of Bucks Row. And people were sleeping within a few yards. A policeman would have been still visible at the end of the street, and there were five others within call. Men were climbing out of bed, getting ready to go to work; others were returning home from Smithfield meat market or from jobs in the docks. But luck was with Jack the Ripper; he murdered Polly Nichols without being heard, and walked off into the dawn. Ultimately, this is one of the most amazing features of the case - the extraordinary luck that never deserted the Whitechapel sadist... as far as we know.

Always a woman ready to die... What does it matter when you're sick of life?

The nickname Jack the Ripper was not invented until shortly before the notorious double murder of September 30th. But the police were intrigued to hear the phrase "Leather Apron" used again and again in connection with the killer. Who was he? No one seemed to be sure. Some people described him as a short, villainous-looking cobbler who carried his clicking knife in the pocket of his Leather Apron. Others said he led a gang that terrorised prostitutes and demanded a percentage of their earnings. Others were of the opinion that he was a maniac who enjoyed frightening women but was probably harmless.

The suspects

The police traced three men whose nickname was Leather Apron. The most likely suspect was a Polish Jew named Pizer, who was arrested on suspicion. His alibi proved to be unshakeable and he was released. Their inquiries came to nothing, but one journalist who visited a doss house in Dorset Street, reported an interesting snatch of conversation.

An old prostitute wandered in, to drink a glass of gin, in the early hours of the morning. The journalist asked her if she was not afraid of meeting Leather Apron. The woman replied "I hope I do meet him. I'm sick of this life. I'd rather be dead." It throws light on the mental state of some of these women, and explains why Jack the Ripper never seemed to have had any difficulty finding a victim, even at the height of the terror. A week after the murder of Mary Nicholls, the murderer found his third victim. And the pattern of the crime is curiously similar to the previous case. Mary Nicholls was turned away from a doss house in Thrawl Street, and went off to seek a "customer". Annie Chapman was turned out of a doss house in Dorset Street by a man named Donovan, the keeper. And like Mary Nichols, the life of Annie Chapman was sacrificed for four pence, the cost of a bed.

Convenient

An extension of Spitalfields Market now stands on the site of the lodging-house from which Annie Chapman was turned away in the early hours of Saturday, September 8th. When she left 35 Dorset Street, she had only a few hundred yards to walk to her death. She turned into Hanbury Street, on the other side of Commercial Street. Halfway down Hanbury Street stands number 29, a barber's shop. (It was still a barber's shop until about 18 months ago; I occasionally went there for a haircut.) In front of this shop, she met a man who allowed himself to be accosted. As it happened, 29 Hanbury Street was a convenient meeting place for a prostitute and a prospective client. A passage runs by the side of the house, with a door at both ends. These doors were never kept closed. At the far end of the passage was a backyard - a yard that looks today exactly as it did 72 years ago, when the Ripper entered it with Annie Chapman. They tiptoed down the passageway and crept into the corner of the yard by the fence. The man moved closer; she was not even aware of the knife he held in his left hand. A moment later, she was dead; the first thrust had severed her wind-pipe. The man allowed her to slide down the fence. He slipped out of his dark overcoat, and bent over the woman. The sight of the blood roused him to a kind of frenzy; for five minutes he remained there, crouched over her. Then he wiped the knife on her skirt, and cleaned some of the blood off his shoes. It was already getting light. He pulled on the overcoat and crossed to the tap that projected from the fence three feet to the left of the body.

False trail

From his overcoat he pulled a bundle, which he soaked in water and used to wash his hands; then he dropped it under the tap. It was a leather apron. As he pulled it out of his pocket, an envelope dropped out too. The man picked this up, tore off its corner, marked with the crest of the Sussex Regiment, and dropped it into Annie Chapman's blood. It would be another false trail for the police. Before leaving the yard, another idea struck him. He searched the pockets of the dead woman's jacket, and removed two brass rings, a few pennies and some farthings, and arranged these carefully by her feet. A few pennies! Annie Chapman had actually possessed just enough money to stay in the lodging house! Did she know this? Or could it be that my reconstruction is wrong, and the Ripper took the pennies from his own pocket, a sort of ironical payment for the pleasure she had given him? An hour went past and one of the inhabitants of the house, John Davies, came downstairs and looked into the yard. The body was huddled against the fence. He rushed to Spitalfields Market, where he worked as a porter, and brought two of his fellow workmen back with him. A few minutes later, the police arrived, and Mr. Phillips, the divisional surgeon, was summoned. His first act was to remove the handkerchief tied around the woman's throat; immediately the head rolled sideways; it was only just attached to the body.

By now, the windows of all the surrounding houses were crowded with sightseers, and some of the inhabitants even charged a small fee for access to their windows. Finally, the body was removed to the mortuary where Mr. Philips discovered that the injuries were even more extensive than in the case of Mary Nicholls. In addition to numerous stab wounds, there were incisions in the woman's back and abdomen. Moreover, a careful examination of the body revealed that certain internal organs had been removed and taken away by the murderer. So also had two of her front teeth - a curious touch that repeated a feature of the murder of Mary Nicholls. At the Inquest, Dr. Philips expressed the opinion that the murderer must have been a man with some anatomical knowledge and medical skill. And the weapon must have been some kind of long-bladed knife, at least eight inches long, which might have been "an instrument such as a doctor would use for surgery." Of all the Ripper murder sites, that at 29 Hanbury Street is best preserved. When I knocked on the door a few weeks ago, it was opened by Mrs. Kathleen Manning, who is now the sole occupant of the house, together with her husband and daughter. (In 1888, 16 people lived in it!)

No details

Mrs. Manning knew that one of the Ripper's murders had been committed there, but she knew no details of the crime. But she told me of how, on one occasion, she showed a friend of her daughter the way to the outside lavatory. In the yard, she mentioned, casually, that Jack the Ripper had committed a murder there. To her surprise, the friend disappeared abruptly into the street, and refused to go back into the house!

Within a hundred yards of this last grim remnant of 1888, blocks of council flats have replaced the insanitary lodging houses and narrow alleyways through which the Ripper escaped. If the Whitechapel maniac could visit his old haunts today, it is doubtful if he could find his way around!

21 Years of Jack the Ripper and the Whitechapel Society

Berner Street in 1909

The most sensational crime night of them all

Children sing and play today on the spot where the Ripper's next victim was killed. It was in the backyard of the International Working Men's Club, 40 Berner Street, where the Ripper began the most sensational night's work in English criminal history. The yard is now a part of the playground of a London council school. No one I talked to in the area even knew Jack the Ripper had committed a murder there. But although the club has disappeared, the upper part of Berner Street still looks much as it did when the Ripper walked down it on the night of 30 September 1888. The story of that remarkable night begins at 1am, when the steward of the club tried to guide his pony and trap into the backyard. He had some difficulty, for the pony was obviously unwilling to enter. The cart blocked the gateway. The man, Louis Deimschutz, dismounted and peered into the darkness, trying to find out what was frightening the pony. He did not know it, but he was very close to death. A few feet behind him, still holding a knife, was the Whitechapel sadist. But Deimschutz was not aware of this, for he saw the body of a woman lying against the wall, and rushed into the club to raise the alarm.

Disappeared

The man who would soon be known as Jack the Ripper clambered over the wheel of the cart and slipped out into Berner Street. A moment later, he had disappeared into an alleyway. Deimschutz emerged from the club, followed by a crowd of men who babbled in Polish and Russian. Someone struck a light. The body was that of a tall woman shabbily dressed; her throat had been cut and one of her ears slightly torn. The Ripper had been interrupted. The doctor who was called, verified that the woman had been killed very recently indeed. At the moment that the murderer walked out of Berner Street into the Commercial Road, a prostitute named Catherine Eddowes was released from Bishopsgate Police Station, where she had been charged for drunkenness at 8 o'clock. Five hours in a cell had not sobered her appreciably; she still staggered as she walked down Bishopsgate towards Aldgate. And the man who had just left Berner Street was walking along the Commercial Road towards his usual haunts. Berner Street was the farthest afield he had yet ventured; it is on the right-hand side as you go down the Commercial Road towards the East India Dock Road, a good half-mile from Commercial Street the Ripper's usual hunting ground. Perhaps he was finding the narrow lanes of Spitalfields too hot for him; policemen in rubber soled boots walked through the alleys, and the tradesmen of Whitechapel also wandered around in bands of "vigilantes" in the hope of catching the murderer. At all events, the Ripper avoided Spitalfields and walked on towards Bishopsgate. And at the corner of Houndsditch he met Catherine Eddowes. After a brief conversation, the two of them turned off to the right, into Duke Street.

In doorway

Halfway up Duke Street there is a narrow alleyway called St. James

Passage; in 1882, it was known as Church Passage. At its far end, lies Mitre Square, which looks today almost exactly as it looked in 1888. On its north side stands a warehouse. The Ripper was standing on the south side of the square, near Church Passage, when PC Watkins walked through the square on his beat; as the policeman walked by, he pressed the woman back into the shadow of a doorway. As soon as the steps were out of earshot, he placed a hand over her mouth, and cut her throat. Exactly a quarter of an hour later, PC Watkins again walked through Mitre Square. But this time a mutilated body lay in the right hand corner, near Church Passage. There was no room for doubt about the identity of the killer. The body had been stabbed and cut unrecognisably: the face had also been cut beyond recognition. And two of the woman's internal organs were missing.

Little time

The murderer had not given himself very much time.

The doctor who examined the body agreed that it must have taken at least ten minutes to inflict so many injuries; besides, the removal of the organs revealed some medical skill. And yet the man walked off without fear into Duke Street, and walked across Whitechapel, into Dorset Street, where he found a convenient sink in which to wash his hands. He had torn off a fragment of the woman's apron, and used this to wash off the blood. Major Smith, of the City Police, actually saw the sink before the bloodstained water had time to drain away. Possibly some noise frightened the killer there, for he hurried away without finishing the wash, and continued to wipe off the blood as he walked towards Aldgate again; he finally dropped the piece of bloodstained apron in Goulston Street, within a short distance of the scene of the murder. Although the Ripper did not know it then, Dorset Street was to be the scene of his most horrible murder, six weeks later. Early the following morning, the Central News Agency received a letter written in red ink, signed Jack the Ripper. It was their second letter with this signature. The first had arrived two days before the murder, and promised "some more work" in the near future. It also promised to clip off the lady's ears and send them to the police. No one took this first letter seriously; it was assumed to be another practical joke. But the second letter altered the complexion of things. To begin with, it arrived early in the day, before the news of the murders was generally known. Secondly, there had been an attempt to cut off the ear of the first victim in Berner Street, and in his second letter the Ripper apologized for not sending it, saying he had been interrupted!

Hysteria

The murder of Annie Chapman in Hanbury Street had caused a sensation; but it was nothing to the furore that followed the double murder. Hysteria swept the country. Sir Charles Warren, the unpopular Commissioner of Police, was bombarded with furious telegrams demanding his resignation. (He did, in fact, finally resign). He was also bombarded with letters full of theories about the identity of the murderer and how to catch him. It is almost impossible to give an adequate idea of the commotion caused by the murders. But the newspapers of the day devoted more space to them than our own journals devote to a royal wedding. The police arrested about a dozen men a day, and released them after questioning. Sometimes, cranks gave themselves up as "Jack the Ripper" - the name had caught the public imagination after the two letters.

Coincidence

The police took some time to identify the two women. The woman who was killed in Berner Street was finally identified as Elizabeth Stride, a Swedish woman who had taken to drink and prostitution after some emotional tragedy. (One story has it that she saw her children drowned on a Thames steamer.) The second victim was less easy to trace, because the mutilations to her face made recognition difficult. There was even a stage at which she was "identified" as an Irish woman named Mary Anne Kelly – an astounding coincidence when one realizes that the name of the Ripper's next victim was Mary Jeanette Kelly. Finally, the evidence of her clothes established that she was Catherine Eddowes, aged 45, and that she had been in police custody only three quarters of an hour before she was murdered.

Now the final question: who was the Ripper?

The most amazing theory of all - was he sent by Russia? There are very few streets in London whose names have been changed because of an evil notoriety associated with the original name. I know of only one in recent years – Rillington Place, the site of the Christie murders.

But there seems no doubt that Jack the Ripper holds a record for altering street names. Bucks Row, the scene of the murder of Mary Nicholls, is now Durward Street; Dorset Street, the scene of his last murder, has become Duval Street; and I have never been able to discover what became of George Street, the site of his first murder. Seventy-two years ago, Dorset Street was a narrow and shabby thoroughfare running parallel with Spitalfields Market in Brushfield Street. On its North side, extending towards the market, was an entry labeled Millers Court. It was in a house in Millers Court that the Whitechapel sadist killed and dismembered his last victim, a 24-year-old prostitute called Mary Jeanette Kelly. Five weeks had elapsed since the double murder; London began to hope that the Ripper had left town. The police and the vigilantes began to relax a little. Then on the morning of November 9th, a man knocked on the door of Mary Kelly to ask for the rent. Getting no reply, he went around to the window and peered through the half-open curtains. What he saw was probably the most appalling sight in London's violent criminal history.

Hysteria grows

The body that lay on the bed had been taken to pieces like a jigsaw puzzle. And the pieces scattered around the room, draped over a picture or piled on the sideboard. The heart lay on the pillow at the side of the head. The hysteria in London reached new heights. At some time after two o'clock on the morning of November 9th, the Ripper had been solicited by Mary Kelly outside her room in

Millers Court. A man named Hutchinson had actually watched the "pick up" and described the man as a "toff", a short, thickset man with a moustache. A short time later, a neighbour heard Mary Kelly singing "Sweet Violets". At 3.10am, the same neighbour heard a cry of "Murder."

And for the next two hours there was silence as Jack the Ripper dissected the body. Then Jack the Ripper left, and the great mystery begins.

What happened?

How did he walk through London in clothes that must have been soaked in blood? Why did he burn a pile of clothes in the grate in Mary Kelly's room? Above all, what happened to the murderer after November 9th?

There is no case in history of a maniacal killer who simply stopped of his own accord. Why did he stop? These questions have puzzled students of crime for the past 70 years. There are theories but no shred of evidence. Is it possible, at this late date, that one day someone will prove the identity of Jack the Ripper? Are there papers somewhere, in police files or in some mental home, that tell the whole story? We come, then, to the theories on the case.

My own conviction is that the Ripper was a sadist who found it impossible to gain sexual satisfaction except by inflicting pain or producing large quantities of blood. It is also barely possible that he may have stopped of his own accord, completely satiated by his final crime. The best known theory of the Ripper's identity and motives was propounded by Leonard Matters. Matters declared, without producing a shred of evidence, that the Ripper was a certain Doctor Stanley, a widower who had been passionately fond of his only son. The son had died of syphilis, contracted from Mary Kelly and Doctor Stanley had then devoted his life to a search for the woman.

He questioned all his victims about her, and murdered them to make sure they kept silent. Finally, after he found Mary Kelly, he ceased to stalk the East End. Matters alleges that Doctor Stanley died in Buenos Aires, and made a circumstantial deathbed confession.

Three poisoned

One of the most popular theories in police circles is that George Chapman was Jack the Ripper. Chapman was actually a Pole whose real name was Severin Klosowski, and at the time of the murders, he was working as a barber in Whitechapel. In 1889, Chapman went to America, returning to London in 1892. During the next 10 years, Chapman poisoned three women with whom he cohabited. There was no motive for the murders: he gained nothing by them; it is almost certain that they were purely sadistic. Chapman was executed in 1903, and Chief Inspector Abberline, who had been in charge of the Ripper investigations, stated dogmatically that Chapman was Jack the Ripper. Certainly the dates correspond closely enough, and Hargrave Adam, who edited The Trial of George Chapman, declares that "Ripper murders" took place in Jersey City while Chapman was living there in 1890. But it is hard to believe that the man who dismembered Mary Kelly could have changed his method to antimony poisoning.

One of the most plausible theories of the Ripper's identity was recently put forward by Donald McCormick in his book *The Identity of Jack the Ripper*. McCormick points out that among the papers of Rasputin, the "Russian monk" who was murdered in 1917, there was a document that claimed that Jack the Ripper was an insane Russian, who had been sent to England by the Tsarist police, with the sole aim of embarrassing the English police. Mr. McCormick unearthed a great deal of evidence to connect the Ripper murders with Russian immigrants in the East End, and particularly with a barber-surgeon, Pedachenko.

Best lead

He claims to have seen an issue of a Russian secret police gazette which reports the death of Pedachenko in a Russian mental home, and mentions that he had committed five murders of women in the East End in 1888. If this piece of evidence is still in existence, it is probably the most definite lead we have to the Ripper's identity.

According to Mr. McCormick's theory. Pedachenko lived in

Walworth, and was helped in his murders by two accomplices. His description corresponds closely with that of the witnesses who claim to have seen the Ripper: a short, broad-shouldered man with a large moustache, well-dressed, with a gold watch chain.

McCormick's theory is the only one that might still be verified. After all, the Rasputin papers must still exist in Moscow archives, and the details of Pedachenko's case are presumably in the files of the asylum in which he died.

If it is ever definitely established that the Ripper was Pedachenko, one of the great mysteries of crime will be at an end.

The East End of Jack the Ripper is disappearing fast, but is still just to be seen in a few alleyways and narrow entries into old buildings. His murders were a product of these slums and of cheap gin, of starving women and four pence a night doss houses. In spite of their "local colour" it will be as well when they disappear forever.

2004
LONDON CORRESPONDENCE: TALES FROM THE STREETS OF WHITECHAPEL

ALAN SHARP

Alan Sharp is the owner/operator of White Rose York Tours, a historical walking tour company in York, England. He is the author of two books in the Grim Almanac series for the History Press. His article appeared in edition number 51 of Ripperologist, and formed the basis of his first book, London Correspondence: Jack the Ripper and the Irish Press

In 1888, the political situation in Dublin was a mess. Two years earlier the Republican politician Charles Stewart Parnell had attempted to take the first steps towards independence from the United Kingdom by introducing a Home Rule Bill to Parliament, with support from the Prime Minister, Mr. Gladstone. The bill was defeated, and subsequently Gladstone lost the General Election of the same year fought almost solely on the Home Rule issue. In 1887, *The Times* of London published a series of articles accusing Parnell and his supporters of the most heinous crimes and of supporting the assassination in Phoenix Park of the Irish Secretary Lord Cavendish and his assistant. The result of these articles was the Parnell Commission, set up by the government to investigate the allegations, which opened in mid-October 1888 at the height of the Ripper scare. Meanwhile the Irish Republican or Fenian

London Correspondence: Tales from the Streets of Whitechapel

Brotherhood, forerunner to the IRA, continued to be a thorn in the side of the British government. Founded in 1858 by James Stephens, the movement published its own newspaper, The Irish People, to get the Republican message across to the masses.

The newspaper of choice for the British bureaucrats who controlled the country from Dublin Castle and the landowning classes who still pledged their allegiance to queen and parliament, was *The Irish Times*. It was a newspaper which had to walk a fine tightrope, presenting a pro-Irish stance that the general populace would find palatable, while not offending the colonial ex-pat ruling classes who made up a large proportion of its readership. For those to whom London still represented the centre of the universe, a daily column by the name of "London Correspondence" kept them in touch with the happenings of the capital city. A mixture of political and social gossip, it attempted to give a fair representation of the mood of the city.

The Ripper has often been incorrectly described as the first serial killer. He was not, but he was the first to become a global phenomenon. The first TransAtlantic telegraph message, a 94 word message of congratulations from Queen Victoria to the new US President James Buchanan in 1858, had taken sixteen hours to transmit. But by the time of the Ripper murders the technology had been perfected and details of the crimes and the victims were appearing in newspapers around the world within hours of their first appearance in their British counterparts. *The Irish Times* covered the case extensively, possibly using the story to deflect attention from problems at home as a kind of "worse things happen at sea" scenario. When I recently began studying these reports and transcribing them for the Casebook website, I began to realise that in "London Correspondence" there was a wealth of information about the mood on the streets of Whitechapel, together with a number of amusing anecdotes connected to the case, many of which I had not come across before.

It all begins quite calmly. The first mention of the Ripper murders appears in the column on 1 September:

You will have from other sources an account of the horrible murder committed last night in Whitechapel, where a woman of 40 was found with her throat cut and the lower part of her body almost hacked to pieces. The aspect of this tragedy noted here is its suggestive resemblance to the atrocity reported about three weeks ago where a woman of like age was found in the open hall of a common lodging house, also with her throat cut and thirty-nine slashes and stabs in different parts of her person. The similarity in many points of these two crimes has stirred again suspicion that both poor women were victims of the same miscreant. We hark back to the time a century ago when "the monster" prowled about London attacking women with a knife, and the theory is that some still more sanguinary scoundrel may now be gratifying a like mania. If so, it can only be hoped that he will speedily experience the punishment of his predecessor.

The monster referred to was most likely Renwick Williams, convicted of malicious assault against one Miss Ann Porter in 1790. Williams was believed to have attacked several young ladies, cutting their clothes and wounding them in various parts of their bodies, although he is not known to have killed.

For the next week, although the newspaper printed a daily report, diminishing in size as each day passed, of the search for the killer, the London Correspondent had other things such as the social merry-go-round, the preparation for the Parnell Commission or the forthcoming opening of *Yeoman of the Guard*, the brand new Gilbert and Sullivan, on his mind. But on 10 September, on the day that the paper gave over almost an entire page of its eight broadsheet pages (four of them taken up with advertising) to the Annie Chapman murder, a report appeared which transported me back in time and made me understand what it must have been like to stand outside No. 29 Hanbury Street that day:

The scene yesterday afternoon at the East End gave an instructive insight into what we might expect in periods of public panic when the crowd loses its head under the pressure of mixed anger and fear, and the popular temper heats to the danger point. The locality in which the butchery of Friday night was committed is also the theatre of the previous three murders charged with good reason

London Correspondence: Tales from the Streets of Whitechapel

Hanbury Street on the Sunday morning following Annie Chapman's murder

to the same hand. It lies off the Whitechapel road, part of the main artery through the vast region lying east of Aldgate pump. There are many dangerous slums in this poorer London, with its million and a half of population - it does not include the entire east - and the district which has been the theatre of such horrible tragedies has always borne a bad name. Anybody who walked in the Whitechapel and its continuation, the Mile End road on a Saturday afternoon when the cosmopolitan multitude, representing twenty nations, are abroad, will see for himself the elements which have brought upon certain districts the character of places to be shunned even in the daytime.

Yesterday at 4 o'clock, the throng in the neighbourhood of the murder numbered thousands. Every one of the heavy forbidding by-streets leading to the spot was packed with the curious and idle - a repulsive gathering it must be owned, for the vast majority represented the human types whose ways and works have earned for this part of the great Babylon its evil fame. These natural denizens were mingled with a better class - working men evidently wasting their Saturday half-holiday in the gratification of a morbid curiosity, with not a few horror hunters who might be carriage folk.

Everybody was talking of one thing, and it was interesting to note how excited all seemed to be.

Even the Cockney, callous through familiarity with daily tragedies of one kind or another, are fairly shocked and scared by deeds more monstrous and terrible than this generation has known. The East Ender is more apt to be staid than respectful over even such subjects as the loss of life by murder, but there was none of this yesterday. The hard and villainous faces which were numerous enough showed something like pity and indignation, and while the assassin, if he was among us, would not have looked peculiar in such a gathering it is certain that if the worst of us - burglar, bully, wife beater, pickpocket, highwayman or worse still though we might be - had our hands upon him we would have lynched him there and then in an honest impulse of avenging justice.

The air was filled with murder. It was the talk, there was nothing else to hear. Men, women and children all chattering at once with deep oaths, and shrill feminine denunciations. The crowd had its nerves strong and its blood up. It was evidently raging in a blind way to go for somebody or something. It did partly indulge this mood, for the evening papers printed an interview with an inmate of the dingy lane called Hanbury Street, who had described a male acquaintance of the murdered woman as of Jewish appearance. The tribe have been in very bad odour here, especially since the revelations of the sweating system. In fact there is a sort of 'Judenhetze' afoot, and the natives, swift to condemn the Israelite on the ground that if he did not murder the woman he is taking the bread of Christian mouths, soon began to exclaim against the chosen people, and to threaten those present. Those were a very considerable fraction of the throng, and being a congruous and choleric race, the whole evening onwards was enlivened with a series of free fights and single combats between Jew and Gentile.

All the time there was a steady movement from every approach upon the scene of the tragedy. This was a very small and grimy yard, occupied by half a dozen stalwart constables who prevented the mob from swamping the place. The sergeant in charge could do nothing to hinder the inmates of the house from turning an honest penny out of the murder. This they did by charging that sum for a peep at the corner where the deed was done and the body lay. The pennies were paid as fast as they could be taken. The entry purchased you fell into single file with the procession of sightseers before and behind, passed two or three feet into the yard, saw some broken cases, a pair of steps and other things, and then in a corner a large irregular dark stain on the ground. Before you had well set eyes on it you found yourself quickly elbowed outside, for the coppers were moving too fast and time was too short to allow you more than a glance for your copper.

A week later, on Monday 17th, another wonderful discovery awaited me. This time it was a lengthy diatribe from a local constable on the newly formed Whitechapel Vigilance Committee. The policeman is not named, but his remarks are highly revealing about the atmosphere which must have existed on the streets between the professional and the amateur law-enforcer:

It won't last a month. They'll get little help - at least no more than anyone else - from our chaps; and if they get interfering with respectable people our men will 'run them in' as a caution for future behaviour. With regard to the roughs, well all I can say is 'they will have a high old time of it' and to the benefit of our men. They can, to use their own words, 'smell a fly copper' - ie plain clothes man; and when they get hold of an 'amateur' or two of them, God help the amateurs! Kicking a regular policeman is a pleasure at any time not lightly to be spoken of, but the chances of 'booting' the head or ribs of an amateur 'slop' will afford a new and indescribable pleasure, and one to be indulged in on every possible occasion. These 'vigilants' will be looked upon as 'copper's noses' or 'copper's narks' - ie police informers - and to use the rough's own words, 'a copper is bad enough, but his nark!' - well, kill him, and that's about what he will get, or something very near it. They have forgotten one thing in their outfit, and that is an 'ambulance' - that will be wanted oftener than truncheons. At least I think so.

Between the Annie Chapman murder and the double event, the mood of the columns remains relatively light-hearted, presented in the tone of the subject Irishman amused at the consternation of his English cousins. The blundering antics of the police are a particular target of his mirth:

An instance of over-zeal on the part of a detective officer formed a topic of gossip in the vicinity of Whitechapel today. Some few of the men at first engaged in the case are now on holiday leave. Their

> places have been filled by comparative strangers from Scotland Yard, who merely report themselves to the local inspectors and proceed upon their duty at the positions allotted them. At two o'clock this morning a man was seen talking to a woman near Great Pearl street. A detective on the look-out considered that he was at last within measurable distance of the real "criminal." Approaching the stranger cautiously he questioned him as to what his business was at this hour. His answers were not considered satisfactory, and certain recriminations led to such unpleasantness that the woman's companion was told he must go to the station. The detective was then somewhat surprised to find that he had arrested a brother officer, who was forthwith liberated upon the production of his warrant card.

On 1 October, as could be expected, the mood of the column was sombre. Unfortunately the author obtained no such coup as in the case of the Annie Chapman murder, and the reports are similar in tone to many published elsewhere. A few snatches and phrases catch the attention.

The opening para graph provides a neat Irish slant on the mood of the Capital:

> Fresh horrors were in store for us this morning and ere the church bells had commenced to ring the sensational news of two fresh murders in the East End had travelled into the far distant suburbs of the metropolis. The panic produced by the dreadful news was widespread and general, and later on when the ghastly details became known the effect on the Londoner can only be likened to the sensation which prevailed in Dublin on the Sunday following the murders of Lord Frederick Cavendish and Mr. Burke.

An interesting comment included later:

> The neighbourhood of Aldgate and Commercial Road is an exceptionally busy one on a Saturday night, and, as a rule, it is some three hours after midnight before the streets are actually quiet.

There is much description of thronging crowds and idle gossip, and the report concludes with an astute and telling observation:

> The feeling among the inhabitants is one of intense excitement and it would be extremely difficult for the police should they make

> *an arrest to get their prisoner safely to the station, owing to the present excited condition of the labouring classes, who form a large proportion of the residents in the locality. Great caution is therefore being taken by the authorities not to state any suspicion of a clue.*

By the following day however the former conversational and whimsical tone of the reports had returned and the correspondent was once again regaling the Irish populace with an amusing anecdote from the mean streets of the metropolis. The police were once again the butt of the joke, and on this occasion a fellow journalist was the central character. The tale was intended to highlight the difference in attitude between the City and Metropolitan police forces.

> *One unfortunate scribe who has been on the look-out for the murderer for several nights past, yesterday, with enterprise hardly to be commended, shaved off his whiskers and, attired in female garb, perambulated the streets frequented by the assassin in the hope that he might come across him. He passed several detectives and was unmolested until getting into Whitechapel Road, when he was pounced on by a quick-sighted constable who charged him with being a man. Seeing that it was useless to deny it, the reporter admitted the fact, upon which he was asked, "Are you one of us?" and was answered in the negative, and it was explained why the disguise had been adopted. The constable, however, took him to the station where the Inspector on duty, after several questions, detained him while inquiries were set on foot, and after a delay of an hour and a half, the officer being satisfied of the reporter's bona fides, liberated him.*

On 8 October, in a thoughtful column, the correspondent mused at length on the effect that the murders were having on the police and the local community:

> *Outsiders have no idea of the manner in which the huge community is affected by this veritable pestilence which walketh in darkness. Servants refuse to venture abroad after dark; their mistresses share the same distrust. Judge of the sheer inconvenience and domestic discomfort resulting in one way or the other. Authority still gropes after the assassin, while we continue to devise more or less idle theories in explanation of the atrocities.*
>
> *It must not be supposed that the terror, real as it is, manifests itself very decidedly to anybody in search of it. The two millions of people*

> living in East London enjoy at least the sense of security which belongs to multitude, and the streets and slums are as crowded by night as well as by day. It seems, however, that the particular theatres of the dozen streets and lanes associated with the recent crimes are wholly deserted by females once night falls.
>
> Nothing is more remarkable in connection with these murders than the sense of impotence - there is no better term for it - which they have spread among the police. Whatever may be the feeling at headquarters or among the officers of the force, the rank and file appear to be in a manner demoralized by the utter impunity with which the crimes have been committed. Talking with some of them last night, they expressed in each case a fear that some fresh atrocity would be committed in their midst before the morning. The men seem disheartened by what is certainly an excusable consciousness of the difficulties which handicap them in dealing with an alert, cool, and crafty miscreant such as the assassin has shown himself to be.

Two days later and the mood has changed utterly again. Now our correspondent seems almost disappointed to have had no new and more terrible atrocity to report in this sexiest of all murder stories for over a week.

> The newsometer again points to "dull" and we are anxiously awaiting a change in affairs. The public has of late been so fed upon sensation that the fare of commonplace cannot content its appetite, accustomed to the daily spice of mystery and murder. As if to highlight this point, the rest of the day's column deals with the retirement of a Scottish judge, the menu for a Shakespeare themed dinner and the unveiling of a monument in Stratford, the arrangements of an annual dairy show, and a report that Sir William Harcourt, having sworn off drink, was now taking a little wine for his stomach!

A timely warning to feminists. It might be wise to look away now to prevent the blood from boiling during any reading of the 12 October column.

> The very latest addition to the maze of recommendations is Miss Power Cobbe's idea of a female detective. This proposal is variously, but, upon the whole, not favourably regarded. We are aware that in other countries women have successfully reversed the hint

London Correspondence: Tales from the Streets of Whitechapel

> to "chercher la feminine," and have shown the keenness of the sleuthhound in running their man to death. The Rus Jerusalem employ female detectives, and so does the director of the "Third Section" in St. Petersburg, the function of the petticoated police being in each case the detection of crime. Up to the present Nemesis in her true sex has not been enlisted in this country in the service of justice - save, perhaps, in such base uses as the conviction of publicans violating the licensing laws or decoys for the adulterators of butter and milk. It is hardly likely that the Home Office or Scotland Yard will entertain the notion.

Amazingly, this is the last item of any note to appear in the column. As has been seen from the English press, the public seem to have lost interest in the case as October wore on and no further salacious developments occurred to provide the gossip-mongers with their juicy tit-bits. Meanwhile the opening of the Parnell Commission was the main subject of discussion for the Irish, and on many days the column failed to appear at all, giving over its space to the extensive coverage of those proceedings which often filled two whole pages of the eight available. On 8 November, the day before Mary Kelly met her untimely end, the *Irish Times* published a special 12-page issue, but with not only the Commission proceedings to report, but also the Landowner's Convention, the US Presidential elections and a Press Conference on the Irish question given by Mr. Gladstone in Birmingham to cover, not one word on the Whitechapel murders appeared in the whole 12 pages.

In fact it was not until the Monday morning, 12 November, that London Correspondence saw fit to comment on the case once more, with a passage which seems highly appropriate with which to finish this article:

> It is amazing how comparatively slight the effect on the public the latest Whitechapel murder has been. People have supped so full with this class of horror that it has palled upon their faculty for sensation, and no more interest is now shown in these familiar butcheries than in ordinary crime. It is an instructive fact that so far as the large force of police on detective and usual duty in the East End have observed the class to which the latest victim, like her six unfortunate sisters, belonged appear to have grown callous to

peril, and are not terrified by the latest warning of their possible fate.

References

The Irish Times issues of 1 September 1888, 10 September 1888, 17 September 1888, 21 September 1888, 1 October 1888, 2 October 1888, 8 October 1888, 10 October 1888, 12 October 1888, 8 November 1888 and 12 November 1888.

Renwick Williams: Newgate Calendar, George Theodore Wilkinson (editor), London: Cardinal, 1991.

Irish Nationalist History and the Parnell Commission: Charles Stewart Parnell, Sean McMahon, Dublin: Mercier Press, 2000.

2005

THE ATTEMPTED MURDER AT MILE END

BERNARD BROWN

This article appeared in edition 3 of The Whitechapel Journal

On Wednesday morning, 28 March 1888, at about half-past midnight (also given as 2.30 am), an attempt was made to murder a young dressmaker or seamstress at Bow. Screams for help were heard coming from No. 19 Maidman Street, a short thoroughfare running off the Burdett Road to the Regent Canal, parallel to the Mile End Road.

A couple of young women, walking in the vicinity, at once rushed up to some constables on duty at the nearby fixed point at Burdett Road, on the corner of Mile End Road, which was manned up until 1.00 am and literally just yards away.

The two anonymous constables, known only as PC 232K and PC 539K of Bow Division, ran to 19 Maidman Street (given by some sources as No. 9) to offer assistance. On their arrival they found a young woman called Ada Wilson lying in the passage, bleeding profusely from a throat wound. Various sources state the victim was attacked upstairs.

Dr. Wheeler, who resided in the Mile End Road, promptly attended and treated her wounds. She was subsequently taken to the London Hospital but was not expected to survive.

Local (CID) Inspector Richard Wildey, (Warrant No. 42848) and Divisional Inspector William Dilworth of the uniform branch, (Warrant No. 49568) were assigned to the case.

Wildey had seniority over Dilworth, having joined the force in March 1862, aged 20, and was attached to S Division (Hampstead) as PC 153S - a vast division stretching out into the Hertfordshire countryside. Dilworth had joined the force, aged 24 in February 1868, as a constable on the salubrious C Division (St. James). At the time of the attempted murder on Ada Wilson, Detective Inspector Wildey had 26 years' service in the force, and had served in the East End on K Division (then known as Stepney Division) since May 1874. Dilworth, on the other hand, with 20 years' service had only joined K Division on 4 February 1888, just over six weeks prior to the attack on Wilson, but had no particular knowledge of the East-End whatsoever, having served on T (Hammersmith) and Y (Highgate) Divisions.

The victim, Ada Wilson, once considered to be at death's door, made a remarkable recovery, and was able to relate the facts of the case to Inspector Dilworth and Wildey. It would seem that on the day in question, she was alone in the house, when she heard a knock on the door and was confronted by a man of about 30 years, and 5 feet 6 inches tall. His face appeared to have been sunburnt, and he had a fair moustache and wore a 'wide awake hat'. The stranger demanded money, and when she refused, stabbed her twice in the neck and ran from the house, leaving Ada for dead in the hall.

Fortunately, the house was also tenanted by Rose Bierman and her mother, who resided upstairs in two rooms. On hearing Ada's screams, Rose rushed downstairs to investigate, and found Ada bleeding from two throat wounds. Rose was just in time to see a young man hastily departing through the front door, and quickly summoned help from two constables (the elusive PC 232K and PC 539K no doubt!), but the fiend had made good his escape.

Unfortunately, the nearest police station at Bow was much further east, near Bow Church than the present Bow Road station (which opened in 1903,) and reinforcements took some time to arrive. A

The Attempted Murder at Mile End

The attack on Ada Wilson

cursory search was made, with no success.

The robust Ada Wilson was finally discharged from the London Hospital on 27 April 1888, almost a month to the day of the brutal attack on her at Maidman Street.

Martin Fido first considered Wilson as an early Ripper victim as long ago as 1987, however other Ripperologists consider the scene of the crime too far east of the Ripper's hunting ground to be seriously included. They disregard, however, the fatal attack on Rose Mylett at Poplar on 20 December 1888, which is much further east than Mile End, but both lying within the jurisdiction of K or Bow Division. In fact, Local (CID) Inspector Richard Wildey investigated both the Wilson and Mylett cases.

Author William Beadle also believes Wilson to have been an intended Ripper victim, and goes so far as to name the assailant as one William Bury, who lodged for a time at Quickett Street, Bow, not far from the Maidman Street incident. His description also fits some of the later Ripper suspects.

On 8 September 1888, nine months after the attack on Ada Wilson, the body of an 'unfortunate' by the name of Annie Chapman was discovered in Hanbury Street, Spitalfields.

One of the witnesses who gave evidence at the subsequent inquest was James Green, who gave his address as 36 Acton Street E, Burdett Road. A spurious connection became apparent, as Ada Wilson and Green resided off the Burdett Road, and possibly knew each other. A perusal of an 1888 map of the Metropolis shows there was no such road as Acton Street E, in the Burdett Road district. There was however, an Acton Street E off the Kingsland Road, running between Haggerston Road and, like Maidman Street, also ran down to the Regents Canal, an ideal escape route meandering as it does behind the houses and wharfs. Fog is always enhanced when near water, the 'cloak of invisibility' attributed to the Ripper by some contemporary newspapers.

Acton Street E8 no longer exists, (now Arbutus Street), although Acton Mews perpetuates the former thoroughfare. Although the other Acton Street E of Burdett Road would also appear to be bogus, Green's address is correctly shown in the *Daily Telegraph* as Ackland Street, (now part of the Burdett Estate).

It is unfortunate that many contemporary newspapers gave only the officers' collar number such as PC 232K and PC 539K, making it virtually impossible to identify such officers who may have important evidence to give before a magistrate or coroner's court. So just who were PC 232K and PC 539K, the first two police officers to attend the attempted murder of Ada Wilson?

PC 232K

A check of the K (Bow) Divisional Ledgers reveal that PC Eli Caunter (Warrant No. 55750) was one of the earliest holders of this collar number. Caunter had joined the force on 26 August 1872, but had relinquished the number nearly a decade later in May 1881, after being transferred to B or Westminster Division as a permanent plain-clothes patrol. He was subsequently promoted to Detective Sergeant on H Division in May 1883, and therefore would have been actively involved in the three canonical cases occurring on the

Whitechapel Division (Chapman, Stride and Kelly).

Nicknamed 'Tommy Roundhead' by his colleagues, Caunter resigned on 5 September 1898 on a pension of £93 6s 8d per annum and retired to live with his wife Susannah at 17 Weymouth Terrace, Hackney Road NE.

With Caunter's departure from K Division in May 1881, his divisional number 232K was re-issued to a PC Roland Saw (Warrant No. 65744), who held it until 14 May 1888, when he was promoted to Sergeant 25G of the adjacent Finsbury Division.

PC Fredrick Graham (Warrant No. 70806) joined the force in June 1885 after having served in the Navy at Sheerness. It was therefore only apt that he should be posted to Thames Division as PC 120TA. Three years later, in May 1888, just two months prior to the Maidman Street incident, PC Graham was transferred to a land division as 232K, a number he was to retain up to his retirement in June 1910. Graham was not, however, the elusive PC 232K reported at the Wilson attack in March 1888, as at the relevant time he was a river policeman! It is therefore fairly certain that the elusive 232K was none other than Roland Saw mentioned above, who had left the force through ill-health on 6 April 1900 with a pension of £44 18s 7d per annum, suffering from general nervous disability and cardiac problems, whilst serving as a station Sergeant on W Division (Clapham).

PC 539K

Having at last discovered the identity of PC 232K Saw, it only remains for the identity of PC 539K to be ascertained. PC William Winter (Warrant No. 65522) joined the Bow division as 539K on 28 March 1881, only to be rescinded at Christmas 1882 when he was dismissed for being drunk on duty!

Perhaps the best known holder of the number 539K is PC John Neal (Warrant No. 59168) who in August 1883, was transferred from the X, or Paddington Division in West London to the K or Bow Division in the East End.

Better known as PC 97J, the constable who discovered Polly

Nichols' body in Bucks Row, Whitechapel on 31 August 1888. Neal exchanged his old number 539K to 97J in August 1886, upon the creation of the new Bethnal Green Division, the latter was therefore not present at the attack on Ada Wilson on 28 March 1888.

Nor was a PC 19J John Jones (Warrant No. 44147), who resigned the same day from the Bethnal Green Division, having joined in August 1863.

The elusive PC 539K on duty at Wilson's assault was in fact a PC Thomas Luckhurst (Warrant 71438), who joined the Bow Division on 29 March 1886 (as 708K) until August that year and the formation of the new Bethnal Green Division, when he acquired the number 539K from John Neal.

Anyone revisiting the attempted murder scene after March 1888, might be taken aback by the new occupant. According to the 1881 Census, No. 19 Maidman Street was uninhabited, however in the 1891 Census, Ada Wilson's apartment was occupied by a constable of the Bow Division, and his wife Fanny.

George Eugene Schulz, a native of Berlin, Prussia, joined the force on 27 April 1885 as a PC on the salubrious C or St. James Division, and later that year in December 1885, as an acting sergeant (A/PS) subsequently 379K, from November 1893. Schulz retired on 13 April 1895, due to rheumatism and defective vision, and was awarded a gratuity of £64 7s 0d per annum. It may be interesting to note that an earlier holder of 379K, a PC Guy compulsory resigned on 22 November 1879 for bringing scandal upon the force by marrying a woman who was a prostitute.

Detective Inspector Richard Wildey now assigned to the Commissioners' Office (CO) resigned in August 1890, on a pension of £153.6s.8d per annum, and went to live in Landseer Road, Bow (later Lawrence Street), rear of the present Bow Road Police station, (opened in 1903) with his wife Anne. Divisional Inspector William Dilworth resigned the year after Wildey, in August 1891, the year of the Coles murder (on 13th February) and retired to No. 20 East Road, West Ham Park, Essex with his wife Patience.

The Ada Wilson case was never solved.

2006
SERGEANT WILLIAM THICK

FROGG MOODY

This article appeared in edition 6 of The Whitechapel Journal

Childhood

"It could so easily be missed, this little chalkland village, as many miles from Salisbury as it is from Shaftesbury and once an insignificant settlement on the Northern rim of Cranborne Chase. The Ebble Valley road follows a winding westward course from Salisbury between the ancient downland ridges of the Shaston Drove and the Ox Drove, but at Broadchalke a spur sweeps around the church to run even deeper past succulent cress beds and heron-haunted trout ponds."

Here, at Bowerchalke, William Thick was born on 20 November 1845. William's first home was at Misselfore Green, Church Street, Bowerchalke and quite close by was the Holy Trinity Church where William's parents, Charles Thick and Mary Shepperd had married on the 14 January 1841. This was to remain the family home for over the next ten years with William and his two brothers, Frederick and Robert, and two sisters, Jane and Ellen, all attending the small parish school (built in 1844) for a fee of one penny a week each. "Many of the parents in Bowerchalke had received little education themselves and could see no reason why their children should be taken from gainful employment in the fields. This was often reflected in the pupils themselves who were dull and unforthcoming in their responses."

Early Employment

"When it is fine and the atmosphere clear you can see from parts of the Chase - that remote wooded downland between Bowerchalke and Sixpenny Handley -right across the chequered Dorset countryside to the Solent. For much of the year, however, the south-westerly gales or the biting cold from the north would have made for a hardier breed than the valley people." On leaving school at fourteen, William gained employment as a carter on the bleak and remote West Chase Farm. Adjacent to the farm was Chase Farm Cottages where William and his family now lived. William's work involved transporting loads of hay and wood by wagon along the steep chalk downs between Chase Farm and Rushmore Down. The work could be extremely hazardous and there are numerous reports of fatalities amongst the Chase farming community at this time. By 1865, another three brothers, Morgan, Charles and George and two sisters, Ann and Alice had arrived. William, now 20, and brother Frederick, 18, were both working as carters with father Charles also working on the farm as an agricultural labourer. Conditions were very harsh with the working day starting at 6.00 am and ending at 5.00 pm, six days a week.

"Around the mid to late 1860s, farming in Bowerchalke was steadily declining. Poor harvests and foreign competition had a disastrous effect on corn prices. More and more arable land was laid down to grass and further decline was caused by a sharp fall in the price of wool." Could this decline in farming be the reason why William escaped the harsh employment of rural Wiltshire and travelled to London? For in 1868, William Thick aged 23 left his family and native Bowerchalke and booked his place where fate would forever link his name with England's most notorious Victorian murderer.

London

On 16 March 1868, William Thick (warrant number 49889) joined the Metropolitan Police. Straight away he was appointed to H

Division - Whitechapel - in London's East End. We can only imagine what was going through the young constable's mind on his arrival in Whitechapel from his rural Bowerchalke. Home now was a dark huddle of sleazy lodging houses, a cauldron of squalor, degradation and misery. This was indeed "a land of beer and blood." Over the next four years, William (now living at Leman Street Police Station) would become familiar with the warren of narrow, gas-lit alleyways and courts that merged with the drab, mean houses. He would also gain an understanding of the low-life criminals and prostitutes who made up this despairing landscape - and all this knowledge would not go to waste in the years ahead.

Particulars of Service

After joining the police in 1868 and spending four years at H Division, William was transferred to B Division (Chelsea) on 4 January 1872. This appointment did not last long and on 18 September 1872 he was transferred back to H Division, and sometime between 1872 and 1873 promoted to Police Sergeant. On 8 July 1878, he was transferred to P Division (Camberwell) before returning to his old stamping ground on 3 May 1886 when he was again transferred back to H Division.

William's Family

Meanwhile, back at home in Bowerchalke (which is still known as the most haunted village in Wiltshire), William's family had moved to Woodminton Farm Cottages and this would remain the home of his mother and father until their deaths in the 1890s. Woodminton Farm Cottages then became the home of Charles and Caroline Kerley, whose son Tom would drown on the *Titanic*. Also, the eldest sister of William Thick married a George Kerly at Bowerchalke. Could William be a relative of a *Titanic* victim? My research continues!

On 4 November 1872, William Thick married Hannah Ellison at the parish church, Whitechapel. This was followed, in February 1873, by the birth of their first daughter, Alice Hannah Thick. At the time, the family were living at 4 Wellclose Square, which is very close to Cable Street. Less than a month later they had moved to 71 Greenfield Street (now Greenfield Road), Mile End Old Town. Strangely, according to evidence given at his trial by Wolff Levisohn, Ripper suspect George Chapman also later resided at Greenfield Street. During the Whitechapel Murders it is believed that Chapman was residing at 126 Cable Street.

William was still in contact with his family back in Wiltshire and in 1874, his brother Morgan (who had been employed in Bowerchalke as a shepherd) made his way to London. Morgan also joined the Metropolitan Police, as PC 161 in D Division, Marylebone, and lodged with William in the East End. William's family continued to grow and in 1876 a son, William Charles, was born, followed by another daughter, Rose, in 1879. The following year, Morgan Thick resigned from the Met (for improper conduct off-duty) and gained employment as a brewer's assistant.

By 1881, William's family had moved to 19 Nottingham Place (now Parfett Street), Mile End Old Town.

On 23 July 1881 brother Morgan married Susan Burland in Bethnal Green church. He eventually took over as landlord of the Red Lion public house in Covent Garden, a position he held for six years. For some reason he lost the licence of this pub in 1888, and moved on to Key Street (now Key Close), Bethnal Green. Key Street was in the vicinity of Buck's Row, and during the Whitechapel murders a labourer named John Hummerstone of 11 Key Street was sentenced to 6 months' imprisonment for savagely assaulting a woman with whom he was living, by striking her with a knife. Morgan was still living in Key Street when he died of pneumonia in 1900 aged just 46.

In 1882, the younger brother of William, Charles Thick, aged 20, decided to try his luck in London and on 5 June 1882, he joined the police force as PC 56 N Division, Islington (Warrant no 66684). He only remained in the police force for five years, resigning on 1 February 1887.

Later that same year, in November 1882, William's daughter Ellen Mary died of measles aged just a year. In 1883 another daughter was born and was named Amelia. This daughter completed William's

Sergeant William Thick

William Thick

family and must have softened the blow of losing baby Ellen, who was named after William's favourite sister.

On 18 July 1886, George, the youngest of the Thick brothers, joined the police force at Vine Street (Warrant no 71266). He was transferred from C Division (St. James') to K Division (Stepney), and finally to V Division (Wandsworth). George completed 25 years service on 13 February 1911 and retired to 17 Grove Street, Barnes, naming brother, ex Police Sergeant William Thick as his next of kin.

The 1891 census gives William's address as 81 Dempsey Street. He retired to this same address on 24 April 1893, and was granted a pension of £93 10 0 per annum. The 1901 census has William employed as a Railway Police Inspector and still living at 81 Dempsey Street and in 1902, he famously met the author Jack London at this same address. Upon the death of his wife Hannah, William moved in with his daughter Alice at Northcote Road in South London. William Thick passed away on 7 December 1930.

Sergeant William Thick and the Whitechapel murders, 1888

William Thick's first major involvement in the Whitechapel murders was during the Annie Chapman inquiry. When Annie was murdered on 8 September 1888, Sergeant Thick examined the body at the mortuary and gave a description of it to Sergeant Edmund Barry. William also took an active part in visiting the common lodging houses around the vicinity of Hanbury Street. Two days later, on 10 September, Sergeant Thick made the arrest of the notorious John Pizer, alias 'Leather Apron.' The action of Thick arresting Pizer is hardly surprising when you consider that the two of them lived just streets apart and had known each other for years. Indeed, with feelings against 'Leather Apron' running high, and most of London's police on the lookout for him, it was Thick who knew exactly where to find him, and that he was known locally as 'Leather Apron.' As it turned out, the police eventually decided there was no case against 'Leather Apron' and they released him after two days in custody at Leman Street police station. The following day Pizer appeared at the inquest of Annie Chapman. This was seen as his chance to clear his name in public. After giving his evidence, Pizer and Thick chatted together until the adjournment. Sergeant Thick then escorted Pizer home.

William Thick remained active in the hunt for the elusive Whitechapel murderer, and when Jacob Isenschmid was arrested in the early hours of 12 September 1888, Thick examined his clothing for bloodstains. He also interviewed Isenschmid's wife, Mary. When Mary gave evidence that Jacob used Mrs. Gerlingher's public house in Wentworth Street, Thick promptly interviewed the said Mrs. Gerlingher, who denied ever knowing the man. Isenschmid was finally cleared when the murderer struck again whilst he was still confined in Grove Hall Lunatic Asylum.

The next murder, that of Elizabeth Stride on 30 September 1888, must have shaken William Thick to the core, for the murder site of Dutfield's Yard, Berner Street, was literately a stone's throw away from his residence at 19 Nottingham Place! Later on the same night, a second victim, Catherine Eddowes was found murdered in Mitre Square, Aldgate.

There are not many details charting Thick's involvement on the actual night of the 'Double Event.' But with William living in and around the area of Berner Street for so long, and with the local arrest of Pizer still fresh in his mind, the Stride murder must have surely taken on an extra significance. A few days later, Superintendent Arnold was still using Pizer's name to help justify the obliteration of a chalked message left on the night of the 'Double Event.' The message, 'The Juwes are the men That Will not be Blamed for nothing,' was found in nearby Goulston Street, and Superintendent Arnold later stated in a report: "in consequence of a suspicion having fallen upon a Jew named John Pizer alias 'Leather Apron' having committed a murder in Hanbury Street a short time previously, a strong feeling existed against the Jews generally, and as the building upon which the writing was found was situated in the midst of a locality inhabited principally by that sect, I was apprehensive that if the writing were left it would be the means of causing a riot and therefore considered it desirable that it should be removed..." As well as the message, the murderer also left a piece of Catherine Eddowes' apron, which he used to wipe his hands as he fled Mitre Square. He then headed back towards Whitechapel, to an area already alerted by the earlier Berner Street murder - an area that was perhaps close to home?

The weeks passed by without further incident and then, on 9 November 1888, the killer struck again. Mary Jane Kelly was murdered in the squalid little room she called home - 13 Miller's Court, Dorset Street. Within an hour of the discovery Sergeant Thick was at the scene of the crime where he quickly engaged himself in making inquiries. After some delay, the door to Kelly's room was forced open and the police entered. Mary Jane Kelly was so savagely mutilated that Sergeant William Thick, and indeed any person who saw what remained of that once attractive young girl must have been affected by it for the rest of their lives.

On 12 November, three days after the Kelly murder, *The Times* reported on some of the problems being encountered by the police:

> *Since the murders in Berner Street, St. Georges, and Mitre Square, Aldgate, on September 30th, Detective Inspectors Reid, Moore and Nairn, and Sergeants Thick, Godley, M'Carthy and Pearce have been constantly engaged, under the direction of Inspector Abberline (Scotland Yard), in prosecuting inquiries, but, unfortunately, up to the present time without any practical result. As an instance of the magnitude of their labours, each officer has had, on average, during the last six weeks to make some 30 separate inquiries weekly, and these have had to be made in different portions of the metropolis and suburbs. Since the two above-mentioned murders no fewer than 1,400 letters relating to the tragedies have been received by the police, and although the greater portion of these gratuitous communications were found to be of a trivial and even ridiculous character, still each one was thoroughly investigated. On Saturday (10th November) many more letters were received, and these are now being inquired into.*

According to Stewart P. Evans and Nicholas Connell in their book *The Man Who Hunted Jack the Ripper*, Superintendent Arnold and Sergeant William Thick later took up an inquiry into one Pierce

John Robinson - named as a strong suspect in the Kelly case by his business partner, Richard Wingate. Arnold and Thick proved, however, that Robinson had left his home in the Mile End Road on 1 November 1888 and was in Suffolk on the night of the Kelly murder.

After Mary Jane Kelly, there were other murders deemed to be in the series of that committed by the Whitechapel murderer, in particular the murder of Alice McKenzie on 17 July 1889.

But, like all the others, this one was also found to be "murder against a person or persons unknown."

Two months later, on 10 September 1889, Police Constable Pennett found a woman's torso under a railway arch in Pinchin Street and again, this location was close to William Thick's residence. Perhaps Inspector Reid had this in mind when he directed Sergeant Thick to 'make inquiries at sheds, houses and places where barrows are kept or let out for hire also at butchers in the neighbourhood of Pinchin Street with a view to gain any information regarding the matter.'

By remarkable coincidence, on 10 September 1889, the same day as the discovery of Pinchin Street torso (and the anniversary of Thick's arrest of Leather Apron), a letter was sent to the Home Office from a H.T. Haslewood of Tottenham. It stated 'I have very good grounds to believe that the person who has committed the Whitechapel Murders is a member of the police force.'

Another letter soon followed and this time the author named the member of the police force that he thought responsible - William Thick!

Sources consulted

Public Records Office; Family Records Office; Colindale Newspaper Archive; Collett's Farthing Newspaper (Bowerchalke); Casebook: Jack the Ripper; *Ripperologist* No. 37; *The Man Who Hunted Jack The Ripper* by Nicholas Connell & Stewart P. Evans; *The Complete History of Jack the Ripper* by Philip Sugden; *The Ultimate Jack The Ripper Sourcebook* by Stewart P. Evans and Keith Skinner.

I would also like to thank Bernard Brown for additional police particulars involving Morgan Thick.

2007

FREDERICK DEEMING: WAS HE JACK THE RIPPER?

DES McKENNA

This article appeared in edition 13 of The Whitechapel Journal

"We judge an artist by his highest moments,
a criminal by his lowest"

George Bernard Shaw

Frederick Deeming is now long forgotten as a contender for the title of Jack the Ripper, and it seems almost all researchers give him the heave-ho, but should he be so easily dismissed? He was perhaps the most inhuman ogre ever to stalk the corridor of nightmare. For years he was a syphilitic who boasted of infecting many women, who bragged that he had killed six men, as well as Elizabeth Stride and Catherine Eddowes. I feel he almost certainly diseased his wife, and rounded things off by strangling her with one of her stockings and slitting her throat, and doing the same to his son and three little daughters. After that, he bashed his last wife on the head six times and strangled her as well! And then he buried his wife and family and later his second wife under the hearth. Jack's victims seem to have been strangled before their throats were cut, so the modus operandi was the same, though obviously Deeming could not crank up the paving slabs to bury them.

He was born in Birkenhead in 1853, and earned his money as a con-merchant and burglar, and was a very successful, extremely rich criminal. He had travelled over much of the world before coming to Rainhill, where he settled in at the Railway Hotel, dressed in an old army uniform. The womenfolk were enthralled by this handsome stranger, who clanked about, medals jangling, and with a ceremonial sword rattling at his side, and who spent his evenings as host to the town, roistering in the Railway Hotel, with the bar flies who were only too happy to drink his money away. He wanted to find, he said, a house for his mythical friend Baron Brook, who was a senior army officer, to reside in, and so he approached Widow Mather, who kept the local newsagents and Dinham Villa - an imposing mansion, which would be suitably impressive - and his eyes lit upon the widow's 25-year-old daughter, Emily! He rented the villa and proposed to Emily who, after a little fluttering, accepted him.

Before he came to Rainhill, he and his family sailed to Australia, where he abandoned them and returned to England, I suspect on the same ship. His wife Marie, stranded and penniless, sang in the streets of Sydney to raise the boat fare. She must have had a fine, strong voice, for nothing else about her would appeal to the passer-by. She was an unprepossessing, if not ugly woman. She traced him to Rainhill, and came barging up to her husband, her four children in tow, and a furious row exploded. He explained to everyone that no, she was not his wife, nor were they his young family; she was, in fact, his sister, and the others were his nieces and little nephew – it was just her little joke. They all went back to Dinham Villa, where he locked the doors, strangled them and slit their throats. Over the next few days, he worked tirelessly, digging a hole under the hearth, dumped them all in it on top of each other, and cemented them over. Then he sauntered away, telling everyone that his jocular sister and family had gone on holiday.

Frederick Deeming and Emily Mather wed in haste - it was less than two months between betrothal and marriage - and they sailed almost immediately for Australia. In a Melbourne suburb, he rented the top floor of a house, in which they had been only a few days, before he murdered his new wife and put her corpse under the floorboards. And then he ran away. A foul smell caused the owner of the house to raise the planks in front of the fireplace, and there he found poor Emily.

Deeming was quickly traced to the other side of the continent, and returned to Melbourne to stand trial, and immediately suspicion turned, in most people's minds, to certainty that he was Jack the Ripper. Cawsay, the officer who brought Deeming back to Melbourne, had many long conversations with him on the ship, as they sailed across the Great Australian Bight, and he and the passengers, with whom he came into contact, were all convinced that he was the Whitechapel murderer. The police authorities would not have entrusted the bringing in of such a high profile suspect to a rookie officer. Cawsay must have been well-respected, experienced and competent to have been given the job, and he would no doubt have been used to the boasting of braggarts, and weighed a man up very accurately, and must have had good reason to think as he did. The lawyers and doctors concerned with the trial, were struggling with the problem of whether he was sane or not, but the press reported that they had "little doubt as to Deeming's identity as to Jack the Ripper..." as he had confessed to most of the Whitechapel murders. Reflecting on this many years later, the Liverpool Echo said that even his two defence doctors claimed that he confessed to the last two killings "and they were both convinced that he wasn't lying."

A fortnight before the trial began, a Melbourne paper had these banner headlines:

JACK THE RIPPER: DEEMING AT ALDGATE ON THE NIGHT OF THE WHITECHAPEL MURDERS.

The report went on to say that a London dressmaker identified his photograph as a man she had known as Mr. Lawson. They had gone walking that night, and arranged to meet the next day, when he was very agitated about the double murders of the night before, those no doubt of Stride and Eddowes. He had, so she said "an intimate knowledge" of their injuries, and the description she gave of Frederick Deeming tallied with the police description exactly.

Frederick Deeming: Was He Jack the Ripper?

Frederick Deeming

None of this can be regarded as proof of Deeming's guilt, but already there is far more to suggest that he might have been Jack the Ripper than there is against many a candidate who is looked upon with a stronger suspicion. At that time, this feeling was taken very seriously, and there are one or two other things which bolster the claim. While he waited to be hanged, he read the Bible, said his prayers, and wrote his confession, which was ordered to be destroyed as it was too rambling and obscene.

But was it destroyed, or did one of the jailers keep it? Here was a man condemned for a horrible murder, who shouted out that he was Jack the Ripper, and those who knew him fervently believed that he was. Did he, in that written confession, repeat that claim? He used several aliases, including Druin, Brewett and Drewett. In 1959, a rumour emerged that an Australian document, "The East End Murderer – I Knew Him" had once been seen, which may have been the two or three pages of Deeming's handwritten confession. And that confession was written by Lionel Druitt, Drewett or Drewery.

Many killers it seems want to confess their evil deeds, but are afraid to do so. When Deeming and Emily Mather became engaged, he threw a party at Dinham Villa, and in front of his betrothed and her mother, he did "a funny little jig" on the hearth in the kitchen. He was literally dancing on the grave of his wife and family in front of his new fiancée. Was he trying desperately to tell them what he had done, but was too afraid and when he met that London dressmaker, the day after the double murder, when he was so agitated, and told her so many details of the killings of Stride and Eddowes, was he trying to confess, yet dared not do so?

The Australian authorities must have had good reason to suspect that he may have been responsible for at least some of those murders, for they sent his death mask to Scotland Yard, in case future revelations showed that Deeming really was Jack the Ripper, and even though Sir Melville Macnaghten in his memoranda firmly fingered M. J. Druitt, as Chief Inspector Donald Swanson suspected Kosminski and Sir Robert Anderson suspected either Kosminski or David Cohen, it was Deeming's death mask that was on display in Scotland Yard's Black Museum for many years, as the face of the Ripper.

Jeremy Beadle remarked to me at the Liverpool conference [2003], that Deeming should be regarded as one of England's greatest murderers as he killed, not for money or expediency, but for the joy of murdering. So why isn't he remembered?

I think it is because everyone was so shocked at the depravity of the man. Poor widow Mather, bereft of a husband, had said goodbye to her daughter, perhaps expecting never to see her again, and in the house that she owned, Dinham Villa, her monstrous son-in-law had slain his secret wife and family. Superintendent Keighley, a doughty and much admired officer from Runcorn Constabulary, who had been drafted in to oversee the exhumations, became positive that

Deeming was the Ripper. Terror gripped the town as passionately as it had gripped the East End of London, and the inhabitants believed with the same fervour as the pragmatic superintendent, that they had been visited by the Whitechapel fiend.

Rainhill has, I suppose, two claims to fame. The first being the Rainhill trials, which took place in 1829. This was a contest to find the best locomotive to open the Liverpool to Manchester passenger line, which was the first successful undertaking of its kind in the world. It was also famous because, on the opening of the line, George Stephenson's Rocket ran down and killed the Home Secretary. The Rocket was the first mechanised vehicle to kill a pedestrian and that Home Secretary was the first of over thirty million victims worldwide to be killed by a motorised conveyance.

But the thing that Rainhill and its neighbour Winwick became most famous for, were two huge lunatic asylums. Winwick was the largest of such hospitals in Europe with over 3,000 patients; while Rainhill had over 2,000, and together, these huge institutions looked after the needs of over 5,000 distressed souls, and were home to hundreds of workers.

Nowadays there are few traces left of those old times. The Railway Hotel where Deeming stayed before renting Dinham Villa, changed its name shortly after to the Commercial Hotel, and within it there is not a single mention of the shameful Deeming. Rainhill Asylum is now gone; the Tudor gatehouses pulled down; the farms and lands, the boiler house and wards, clinics and doctors accommodation all gone to housing estates. And the same fate befell Winwick. Gone is the great clock tower which was a landmark for miles around. The hospital was demolished, and only the lovely Victorian chapel, which is now a day nursery, remains.

Dinham Villa was pulled down after the unearthing of Deeming's wife and children, and the kitchen and the cement floor, under which they were buried, was taken to Madame Tussaud's. After that, the house fell into disrepair through souvenir hunters taking away mementos from the fabric of the building.

Widow Mather's newsagents shop was pulled down some years

ago, to make way for a small shopping mall, and the grave where Deeming's family now lie is hard to find. They were reburied in the graveyard of St. Ann's Church of England Parish Church, and each attendant at the service was given a memorial card with the names and small quotation to remember them by: Marie Deeming, the mother, aged 30 years; Bertha, the eldest child, aged 9; another Marie – the second child - aged 7; Sidney Francis Deeming, his son, aged 5; and his little daughter, Martha Lila aged 18 months.

I suspect that the same remembrances and quotations were inscribed on their headstone below which they lie in greater tranquillity than they did when Deeming threw them on top of each other under the hearth in Dinham Villa, but that peace was interrupted over 20 years ago when someone crept along and uprooted the headstone and stole it away. Nobody knows who did such a thing, but one of the church fathers at that time was strongly suspected. His reason can only be guessed at, but personally I think he wanted to erase every trace of Frederick Deeming within the town of Rainhill.

Such is life – and death.

Works Consulted
The Murders of the Black Museum – Gordon Honeycombe
Jack the Ripper Summing Up and Verdict – Colin Wilson & Robin Odell
The Jack the Ripper A-Z – Paul Begg, Martin Fido & Keith Skinner
Lauceston Examiner – March 21st 1892
Liverpool Weekly Post – April 30th 1892
Liverpool Echo – March 29th 1991
Rainhill Public Library – (Various conversations with the staff)
Saint Helens Reference Library – (Help from the Chief Librarian)
Madame Tussaud's 'Chamber of Horrors' – (Advice from Pauline Chapman)
The Murderer's Who's Who – JHH Gaute & Robin Odell
Liverpool Colonade – Richard Whittington-Egan

2008

WHO WAS ANNIE MILLWOOD?

MARK RIPPER

This article appeared in edition 22 of The Whitechapel Journal

In their recent book *The London of Jack the Ripper Then and Now*, Robert Clack and Philip Hutchinson speculate that they have found Annie Millwood, argued (by some other writers) to have been an early victim of the brutality of the Whitechapel Murderer. Put briefly, Annie was admitted to the Whitechapel Union Infirmary on 25 February 1888, having been stabbed. In fact, the assault, perpetrated by a man she described as a stranger, was an intense one, and the damage serious - Annie had been stabbed a number of times "in the legs and lower part of the body" with a clasp knife.[1] Although the record does not mention the geographical location of the attack, Annie had previously been resident (we do not know for how long) at a lodging house on White's Row, to the south of, and running roughly parallel to, Dorset Street. When, on 21 March, she was discharged from the Infirmary, she was delivered into the care of the South Grove Workhouse, just south of the Mile End Road, and there, ten days later, suddenly and unexpectedly, she collapsed and died. At the inquest, Wynne Baxter recorded the cause of death as the "sudden effusion into the pericardium from the rupture of the left pulmonary artery through ulceration". In other words, she was probably ill before she was stabbed, and, the stab wounds having begun to heal, it was her illness which, in the end, killed her. The

Coroner Wynne Baxter

temporal proximity of the stabbing and Annie's death was considered by the coroner's jury to be nothing more than a coincidence, the former having no causal influence upon the latter. Two brief reports of the inquest, which were carried in the *East London Advertiser* and the *Eastern Post and City Chronicle*, her details given on admission to the Infirmary, and her death certificate, issued in response to the inquest's findings, have, thus far, provided more or less the entirety of our knowledge of Annie Millwood.[2]

Searching without reward for any further sign of Annie, Clack and Hutchinson identify a Fanny Millwood, resident in Bath Row, just north of the Euston Road, at the time of the 1881 census, and suggest that, when an Annie Millwood enters the historical record later, in 1888, via the unhappy medium of the register of the Whitechapel Union Infirmary, the two women should be considered to be the same person. Some of the details and circumstances which they provide appear to support this line of reasoning, and I will leave the reader to examine these in Clack and Hutchinson's excellent book;

but at the heart of their thinking about Annie Millwood is the idea that, as they put it, "it is likely that history has incorrectly recorded her name and we are looking at an attack upon a woman named Frances Millwood".[3] It is this position which I find difficult to sustain. In this article, I intend to present an alternative Annie Millwood, one whose credentials are, I think, more compelling, and whose presence in the historical record can indeed be properly traced.

From information given on her death certificate and in her admissions entry at the Infirmary, the world has understood since her modern proposal as a victim of Jack the Ripper that Annie Millwood was the 38-year-old widow of Richard Millwood. Richard was, the certificate says, a soldier. Fanny Millwood of Bath Row also had a husband named Richard, but he, at least in April 1881, seems to have been a decorator. Clack and Hutchinson make the perfectly reasonable suggestion that this Richard, who fails to appear in the censuses for 1861 or 1891, could fit the facts: perhaps overseas on military duty in 1861, perhaps back in England but earning his living in a different way in 1881, perhaps dead by 1891, he may have left Fanny widowed before the attack in February 1888.

As Clack and Hutchinson are (quite correctly) aware, the recording of names in Victorian England - by busy census enumerators, by busy staff in infirmaries, by the part-literate, on behalf of the illiterate, unable to correct an error - is an often unreliable affair. Phonetic approximation, however, is sometimes a way into records which might otherwise remain unexamined. Annie and Richard's surname, Millwood, offers a range of plausible approximations: was she really perhaps a Milward, or a Millward, or a Milwood? And, if she was, could she not have been really an Annie, not a Fanny?

On 10 June 1872, at St Luke's, Chelsea, Richard Milward married Annie East Perry. Richard was thirty-eight; Annie described herself as twenty-five. He was a bachelor at the time of the marriage, she a spinster. He gave his profession: soldier. Both were resident at 12 Charlotte Street. Richard's father was Thomas Milward, a farmer, now deceased; Annie's father was Thomas Perry, he too deceased, thought by his daughter (perhaps, as we shall see, somewhat ingenuously) to have been a solicitor.

Richard himself makes only fragmentary appearances in the historical record. He was christened on 25 May 1834, in Epperstone, Nottinghamshire, the son of Thomas and (an unusual spelling in itself, perhaps suggesting Scottish ancestry) Elizabeth Milward; his entry, aged seven, in the 1841 census, suggests that he was the eldest child of what appears to be his father's second marriage. As he reported on the 1872 marriage certificate, Richard's father, Thomas Milward, was a farmer. Richard himself, however, seems to have been less than committed to the static lifestyle of farming. Setting his sights further afield, he was, in 1851, resident in a lodging house in Sheffield with his elder brother Thomas, and what may very well be their cousin Henry. Thomas fils and Henry are policemen; Richard is described as a sailor. Hereafter, until his marriage in 1872, we see nothing of him, although his early experiences at sea had, apparently, crystallised into formal military service at some point in between.

Annie East Perry is slightly easier to detect. Her birth certificate shows that she was born on 27 February 1844 in Little Queen Street, running south off High Holborn, in the West End. Her mother, Elizabeth Perry (there may be an illegible middle name on the certificate, obscured by an ink blot), was probably born in Greensted, in Essex, on 17 January 1810, the daughter of Thomas and Ann Perry. At some point - it is not clear precisely when - Elizabeth had found her way out of the rural seclusion into which she was born, and into the bubbling crucible of London. Then she became pregnant.

The identity of Annie East Perry's father, however, remains something of a mystery. Elizabeth, who reported her daughter's birth in March 1844, when Annie was a few weeks old, named the father of the child as Thomas King, a servant, but speculating about the identity, and even the historicity, of this character seems redundant. There is little evidence that King was a significant figure in baby Annie's life. The impression of him which she gave at the time of her marriage strikes a dissonant chord, apparently mistaking not only his profession, but even his surname. The figure of "Thomas Perry", solicitor, father of Annie, seems likely to have been, originally,

Who Was Annie Millwood?

Elizabeth's fantasy.

It may be that Elizabeth explained the absence of a visible paterfamilias to a young Annie in terms of his (presumably) tragic death. A more probable explanation would seem to be that Elizabeth, alone in London and detached from her family, had been making ends meet through prostitution, and that she herself was unsure of the identity of Annie's father. If a Thomas King had existed, and if he and Elizabeth had conducted a relationship, of whatever sort, then, in 1844, he may have seemed the obvious choice for inclusion on Annie's birth certificate; but it is fairly clear that, by the time Annie started asking questions about her own identity, King was nowhere to be seen. Stripped of options, but still keen to present the façade of social respectability to her daughter, Elizabeth adjusted and readjusted the facts. She intended to imply that she and Thomas had been respectably married; but, if they had been, why would his surname be King? For Annie's benefit, Elizabeth may have altered it in the re-telling, making him a Perry, and thereby making Perry her "married" name. No trace of any such marriage seems to exist, and only Annie's maternal grandparents might have seen through the conceit; they, however, were too distant from their daughter to give her cause for anxiety. And, since Thomas was by now at least in part a fantasy figure, why not make him - not a servant - a solicitor... Indeed, were they not living on the edge of London's legal district? The jarring unreality of this account, which surely tries too hard to present itself as believable, may sometimes have troubled Annie: the area around Little Queen Street, although a stone's throw away from the chambers of London's most distinguished legal professionals, was described by *The Times* in 1841 as "very confined and populous", crowded with the poor, and Annie and her mother were not obviously the products of a healthy relationship with a practising solicitor, now regrettably deceased.[4] Still, perhaps the explanation, for all its faults, seemed more comforting than the unspoken truth. In 1851, Elizabeth and Annie were living at 5 Tonbridge Street, Elizabeth claiming to be (by coincidence) a thirty-eight-year-old widow, and (by trade) a seamstress. By 1861, Annie was no longer at home. Elizabeth was living at 20 Brunswick Street, which was, like her previous known address, in St Pancras; she now understood herself to be forty-five, and, old habits perhaps dying hard, still reported herself to be a widow.

Annie, meanwhile, seems to have clung to the fictions of her father while she began to make a life of her own. Meeting Richard Milward, a man fairly significantly her elder, but not as much as she made out on her marriage certificate, may have allayed any fears of being, as it were, left on the shelf. His seniority and responsible occupation may have resonated with the idea of the mythical middle-class father with tales of whom she had been brought up. Little can be said about their marriage, however: the evidence is simply not available. Records of Richard's death cannot be traced. Annie's retention of his surname after his death may suggest that whatever time they shared together was happily spent. She obviously mentioned him at the time of her admission to the Infirmary, having experienced, we can reasonably suppose, the real turbulence of a real widowhood, the symptoms of which her mother had probably only feigned.

It is hard to imagine that anyone ending up in a lodging house in White's Row in 1888 - even someone coming from low beginnings, as had Annie - had got there through choice. After the death of her husband, things may have begun to unravel for Annie. Drink and prostitution were linked phenomena in the lives of Jack the Ripper's victims, and it is often, and not unreasonably, supposed that these had played their part in Annie's later life too. Certainly, in February 1888, she found herself in a situation in which she was stabbed over and over again by a man whom she claimed not to know, a man who kept a clasp knife about his person. The crime was not witnessed. Good sense might have suggested to Annie that clandestine encounters with unfamiliar men, with their built-in potential for violence, were generally best avoided. If our limited understanding of her attack is accurate enough, then the idea that Annie was prostituting herself is fairly easily sustained.

It was inevitably an unhappy way to end a life which had probably felt throughout only a dappled happiness: occasionally glimpsed, and soon occluded. Her marriage seems likely to have been one of the happier episodes, although no children appear to have resulted from it. Annie's decline after Richard's death has almost deterministic overtones, a repetition of the desperation into which her mother fell, similarly abandoned by men, except where money was likely to change hands. Through all of this, however, some inextinguishable flame – of hope, or just of acceptance – may have continued to burn. Annie died, the *Eastern Post* said, while "engaged in some occupation" at the rear of the workhouse, her life having gone full circle, from the poverty of Little Queen Street, to the apparent satisfaction of marriage, the grief of widowhood, the violence of Spitalfields, and the meaningless drudgery of the South Grove workhouse.[5] But she "had never complained of feeling unwell", Thomas Badcock, Master of the Workhouse, told the inquest; indeed, she "always seemed in excellent spirits".[6] It was probably too easy for Workhouse masters to say such things at inquests, and it was probably reductive when they did so, but, in the absence of anything else, this would seem to be as close as we are likely to come to a contemporary appreciation of Annie's character.

Lastly, what of her role within the story of Jack the Ripper? Her case has been useful to some theorists – those who favour Cutbush, for example, often see the attack on Annie as consistent with his modus operandi – and, in equal measure, unhelpful to others. At the time, the coroner's jury found no criminal liability against any person in the matter of Annie's death, and the police did not consider her case (if they were aware of it at all) to be connected to the sequence of murders which followed in and around the same locality over the late summer and autumn of the same year. Her modern introduction to the Ripper argument, while it can be understood to contribute to our understanding of the social milieu in which the crimes were committed, can equally be argued to divert the focus of study from the demonstrable facts. However, with the new details which have come to light about her – if one accepts the identification of this alternative Annie Millwood, Annie Milward – she is, perhaps, more appreciable than she has been in the past, and restored, as so many of the other tragic characters of the story have been, to a more sympathetic understanding.

Notes & References

1   *Eastern Post and City Chronicle*, 7 April 1888
2   *East London Advertiser*, 7 April 1888; *Eastern Post and City Chronicle*, 7 April 1888
3   Clack, R. and Hutchinson, P., *The London of Jack the Ripper Then and Now*, 2007
4   *Times* (London), 8 October 1841
5   *Eastern Post and City Chronicle*, 7 April 1888
6   *East London Advertiser*, 7 April 1888

Post-script 2016: Robert Clack and Philip Hutchinson were generous enough to amend the text of their book in subsequent editions, mentioning the research presented in this article. I feel now that this response was more well-mannered than I deserved. The tone which I rather naively took in this article was unnecessarily confrontational and forceful, and subsequently a matter of regret on my part. I thank them both for their patience and humility in this matter. MR

2009
A TANGLED SKEIN?

DAVE CUTHBERTSON

This article appeared in edition 27 of the Whitechapel Journal

In the autumn of 1888, two families - the Strides of Kent and the Perrens of Wiltshire - were declared by a London coroner Wynne Baxter at an inquest to be linked in a comedy of errors.

The inquest was for one Elizabeth Stride, killed on September 30th 1888 in what was soon known as the Double Event. That night, an unknown killer killed two women and during that weekend a letter and a postcard gave him a name: Jack the Ripper. Remarkable in itself, that this summation at the inquest into one of Jack's victims was described by Ripper researcher James Marsh in a lecture at the Princess Alice as 'a tangled skein' with possibly more to it than meets the eye.

During the inquest two conflicting identifications were made of the victim: Mary Malcolm believed the body to be Elizabeth Watts, her sister from Colerne in Wiltshire, whereas Michael Kidney and several others believed it to be Elizabeth Stride from Sweden, widow of John Thomas Stride.

Before looking at the Comedy of Errors listed by the coroner Wynne Baxter let us compare what is now known about both the Stride and Perren families.

Mary Malcolm dreams that her sister kissed her at the excact moment of her death. It proved to be a case of mistaken identity

The Stride family

John Thomas Stride was born in Portsea in 1821 and christened in 1823. The Stride family had originated in Plymouth. His father William, in 1861, lived in a street called Stride's Row as a proprietor of houses (in 1851 he had been a shipwright in the Dockyard). The children appear to have been of a nonconformist background.

Edward Stride was christened in April 1823 in the White Chapel (Wesleyan), Sheerness. Within three weeks John Thomas was christened in St Mary's, Portsea. Charles Stride was christened at the White Chapel in June 1825, then Daniel Elisha was christened in 1834 in Sheerness (Bible Christian Sheerness Circuit).[1]

Census information tells us there were other children: Frederick (b. 1830), Daniel (b. 1835) and Sarah (b.1838). Charles, brother of John Thomas, later fathered one Walter Frederick Stride, who was to be a witness in the inquest of Liz Stride in 1888.

A Tangled Skein?

An important thing to note about the family is that they nearly all seem to have been involved in dockyard work.

Edward Stride was a surgeon and general practitioner (not registered with any College of Surgeons) who died in 1881.

However, in 1841 there is another male Stride in the house - William James Stride. He was stone deaf. The 1841 census is the one in which no notice is taken of family relationships. In every census after he is always in a different household, so there is no census link given to the rest of the family. However, his father was William Stride according to his wedding certificate.

In November 1854 he married a widow, Mary Ann Robinson, nee Martin. He was recorded as a 37-year-old labourer. His father William was a shipwright. Mary Ann, 36, was a schoolmistress. She later died and by 1881 he was listed as a widower, a retired shipyard labourer and a pensioner in a mission in Fieldgate Street - the building in which the Salvation Army first produced *The Warcry*.

William died in 1882 and left property to the Secretary of the Salvation Army.

By 1871 nearly all of the Stride family have left Sheerness. John Thomas Stride was in London. In 1869, whilst living at Munster Road, Hampstead, he married Elizabeth Gustaffsdotter of 67 Gower Street. Born in Sweden, she came to England in 1866, possibly moving to London only months before the marriage. Although Elizabeth told people she had had nine children and many of them died in the *Princess Alice* disaster of 1878, no trace of them was ever found. Wynne Baxter, the coroner, pointed out that subscriptions for the victims of the disaster showed no-one called Stride.

What is known is that by 1871 John Thomas Stride, a carpenter, was living at 178 Poplar High Street with Elizabeth. No children.

They ran a coffee house in Chrisp Street, Poplar. The marriage began to break up. Elizabeth had begun applying for relief individually, but they were still together in the 1881 census - again with no children in the household. John Thomas died in 1884.

She then took up with Michael Kidney, who identified her at the inquest.

The Perren family

A major area of confusion is that Mary Malcolm's history for her sister was immediately, thanks to the Central News Agency, contradicted by the sister herself.

Both sisters have different versions of their own family history. Their father was Aquilla Perren. Aquilla was born about 1808 in Monmouthshire. He had several siblings including Aminter (b. 1804), Amariah (b. 1812) and Arauna (b. 1815).

In 1832, Aquilla married Martha Dodd in Bristol. They had several children: Thomas (b. 1833), Matilda (b. 1835), Clara (b. 1838), Elizabeth (b. 1840), Mary (b. 1842), Martha (b. 1849) and James (b. 1849).

According to *J G Harrod and Co's Directory* of 1865:

> Colerne is a parish and village about 8 and ½ miles WSW of Chippenham 2 NW of Box station, and 6½ NE of Bath, in the hundred and Union of Chippenham, North Wilts. The population in 1861 was 1040.[2]

The List for the Gentry has only six names, one of which is Mrs. Caroline Perren. The Commercial List includes three more Perren family members - Aruna Perren and Frederick Perren, both farmers, and William Perren of Widderton Mill, a paper manufacturer and farmer.

The Perren family seems to have been well spread out in terms of the local pecking order from gentry to pauper. As the years passed they spread out away from the area.

Mary Malcolm's own life is not clear-cut. In 1861 she and her sister Martha are both listed as teenage servants in Bath, in the household of Edward Thorp at 8 Daniel Street. In the 1881 census, she is the wife of Andrew Malcolm in the household of Augustus Delamare, a 73-year-old ink maker, at 47 Baldwin's Gardens in St Andrews, Holborn. Augustus is listed as her father, and Andrew Malcolm is his son-in-law. The married couple seem to have stayed close to the area - in 1888 they were at Eagle Street, Red Lion Square; in 1891, at 3 Fox Court, and in 1901, a few hundred yards further north.[3]

A Tangled Skein?

Despite what is written in the 1881 census, there is no marriage recorded of an Andrew Malcolm to a Perren or a Delamare. However, in 1872 on August 13th, Andrew Fell Malcolm married one Mary Gawen. She is a 30-year-old widow living at 16 Southampton Row, the daughter of Aquilla Gawen, deceased. Andrew is recorded as a 23-year-old tailor living at 3 Little Queen Street, the son of John Malcolm, also a tailor.

The witnesses were Augustus De la Mare and Adolphus Frederick Hatton.[4] Augustus is likely to be the head of the household given in the 1881 census, who was called her father.

However, note a Mary Gawen a 27-year-old housemaid, born in Colerne, Wiltshire, in 1871 living at 1 Widcombe Crescent, Lyncombe, Bath, in the household of Joseph Dallamar, a 64-year-old landowner from London. It seems possible that, considering there is no record of Aquilla Perren's death, he changed his name. He was roughly the same age as Augustus. The name Delamare has many variants and Augustus Delamare is very difficult to trace.

Mary Perren was somewhat imprecise when dealing with census enumerators, police and church officials.

Mary Malcolm's claim that the victim was her sister was definitely wrong, almost immediately contradicted after the Central News Agency and other reporters tracked down her still-living sister Elizabeth to 5 Charles Street, Tottenham. Mary had been meeting a woman claiming to be her sister regularly for about five years and helping her out. Mary Malcolm said her sister knew adulterously - her first husband Watts being still alive - a man called Dent who kept a coffee stall in Poplar. He died on St Paul's Island about 1885. Also, her sister was nicknamed Long Liz.

> She came to me every Saturday, when I gave her two shillings. She did not come to me on Saturday last, at which I was surprised. The Thursday visit was an unusual one. She had not missed coming on a Saturday for three years. She used to come to me at four o'clock in the afternoon. She used to meet me at the corner of Chancery Lane. I was there last Saturday from 3.30 until 5 p.m. but she did not turn up. On Sunday morning, when I read the paper, I thought that as my

sister had not turned up on Saturday it might have been she who was murdered.

Apparently, a naked baby was left by Long Liz on Mary Malcolm's doorstep. "The child is now dead." The father was a policeman.

Then Mary's real sister, Elizabeth Stokes, turned up to refute her tale. A telegram from one "x, y, z", along with a letter sent from Shepton Mallet which was published in newspapers, said that her first husband was still alive.

There are two fascinating mysteries surrounding Elizabeth Perren: the paradoxes surrounding her second husband and her stay in Fisherton Asylum.

In 1861, she is living in Bath at 84 Avon Street, in the household of her cousin Antonio Perren, a 44-year-old labourer born in "Genfax", Italy.

On 3rd January 1864 at the Bristol Register Office Elizabeth, aged 24, married Edward William Watts, a 28-year-old wine merchant. She named her father as Aquilla Perren, deceased.

The children of Edward and Elizabeth Watts were Alice Watts, christened in Colerne in September 1865, and Edward George Watts, christened in July 1866. In 1871 both children are registered as living in the Colerne household of their uncle, James Perren (Elizabeth's younger brother). Edward Watts had emigrated to America, and she believed he had died there.

By Elizabeth's own account, the Watts family kept the children. When she tried to get them back she was put in Fisherton asylum. Fisherton House, Salisbury, was maybe not ideal. According to Molly Whittington-Egan, Dr. Forbes Winslow believed it was there that an official visitor was killed by an inmate driving a nail into his skull. Also, "it was used from 1850 to 1872 for 'harmless' criminal lunatics from Bethlem."[5]

Finally, removed by the relieving officer of Bath, Elizabeth moved to Walmer near Deal in Kent.

Here she met and in 1870 married her second husband, Joseph Sneller. Joseph has a naval career so colourful it will be best dealt

A Tangled Skein?

with in the footnotes. His love life is interesting enough.[6]

It was whilst serving on *HMS Victory*[c] as a private in the Royal Marines that on 27th January 1867 in Portsmouth he married Caroline Preston of 6 St Mary's Street, the daughter of labourer George Preston. In 1870, recorded as a widower, he married Elizabeth Watts in St. Andrew's Church, Deal. He gave his address as 10 Lower Street, Deal, and his father, William, deceased. Elizabeth is recorded as a widow, the daughter of Aquilla Perren.[7]

In the 1871 census, John Sneller, seaman RN, is listed as living at 54 Lucknow Street, Portsea with his wife Caroline and daughter Caroline, who was born in 1870/71. A sister, Ellen Jane, was born in 1876/77.

Reports of his death by both Perren sisters appear to be untrue.

The reference work by W P Gossett, *Lost Ships of the British Navy*, lists a shipwreck in 1871 at St Paul's Island involving the *Megaera*, but no deaths.[8] Sneller's service records show that in June 1871 the ship *Megaera* took him out to Australia.[9]

Sneller also appears in a later census. In 1901, John and Caroline, both born in Deal, were living at 79 Orchard Street, Southsea, Portsmouth. John was a club porter. They also had a 16-year-old son, a shipwright apprentice born in Boxmoor, Herts.[10]

A recent *Casebook* post asked if Elizabeth Perren Watts/Sneller/Stokes was a bigamist. This may be because of a telegram she received during the inquest from "x,y,z", which said Watts was still alive. There's no evidence known so far to say that he was or wasn't alive. But her second marriage was definitely dodgy!

Sneller married Elizabeth as a widower. His first wife was Caroline Preston, but the first child was born after he married Elizabeth. He had one wife in Deal, one in Portsmouth. Elizabeth may not have been a knowing bigamist, but he was. We don't know if the story of the *Megaera* shipwreck in 1871 was used by the navy or Sneller's friends, or Elizabeth herself to end her second marriage. If her first husband was dead and the second marriage was unreal, then she may have felt free to marry again.

She then stayed at Peckham House, a private asylum started by two doctors.

> I was put in the Peckham Lunatic Asylum, under Dr. Stocker and Dr. Brown, because I endeavored to gain possession of my two children, whom I have never seen or heard of since they were taken from me. The Lunacy Commissioners afterwards pronounced me to be sane and I was again discharged perfectly destitute.

Doctors Stocker and Brown had both previously been based in a Poplar asylum. Dr. Stocker may have been an in-law of the extended Watts family.

Elizabeth appears to have stayed in London, and on 15th December 1884 she married Joseph Stokes, a bachelor, at St Andrews, New Kent Road, Newington in Surrey. She was recorded as a widow. Both were hawkers. If her second marriage had been lawful and Sneller was dead, surely she should have married as Mrs. Elizabeth Sneller?

In 1891, Joseph and Elizabeth Stokes are both together in Woolwich at 1 Lewis Place - he was 46, from Stroud in Kent and still a bricklayer's labourer.

In his summation of the evidence given at the inquest of Elizabeth Stride, coroner Wynne Baxter listed the unlikely series of coincidences in the past lives of the victim Elizabeth Stride, as identified by her companion and friends, and the still-living Elizabeth Perren, who turned up in court protesting against her sister's story.

Firstly, both women had a limp. Secondly, there was, according to Michael Kidney, a facial similarity, between Elizabeth Perren and his girlfriend Liz Stride. Thirdly, both had been in the coffee trade in Poplar. Mary Malcolm had said that her sister had a coffee stall with a Mr. Dent. There was a Mrs. Dent who owned a coffee house but no link between her and Elizabeth Stride. The Strides - John Thomas and Elizabeth - definitely had at least two coffee houses in Poplar.

The scandalous behaviour concerning a police constable - adultery, drunkenness and illegitimate children - all seemed to be in the mind of Mary Malcolm. However, there are three policemen who can be linked to this tangled skein concerning the Stride and Perren families:

PC Walter Stride

Walter Frederick Stride was born in March 1858 in Union Street, Blue Town, Sheerness, the son of Charles Stride, a shipwright in HM Dockyard and Hannah nee Wales. Walter joined the Metropolitan Police in 1878, and had married Sarah Rebecca Mercer from Hull a year earlier. At Stride's inquest he testified that he last saw his uncle John Thomas several years previously. No known links to Whitechapel or Liz Stride.

PC John Watson

The wine merchant Watts family of Bath intermarried over the years with Southby, Bennett, Watson families. It's possible that one of Elizabeth Perren's children lived at one time in London within part of this extended network. In 1881, PC John Watson, a 25-year-old from Buxted in Sussex, was living in Great Pultenay Street, Golden Square, with his wife Ellen, a mantle maker. One of his wife's two assistants was 16-year-old Alice Watts, born in Bath, probably the daughter of Elizabeth Perren. By 1891, the mantle makers have gone and he and Ellen have a daughter named Evelyn. His whole police career from 1879 to 1905 was in C Division, St James'.

Did Alice, 23 in 1888, ignore the publicity about her mother living in London and get in touch with Elizabeth? Or did mother and her children never get reunited?

Daniel Healey

Not involved in either the life of Elizabeth Stride or the Perren sisters, his name crops up when investigating the existence of any children born to John Thomas and Elizabeth Stride.

He was the uncle of one of the few Stride children who in the 1871 census was both;

1) not living with parents
2) born after 1866, when Elizabeth entered England (we know when Elizabeth got married but not when she and John Thomas met).

Daniel was an Irish-born police constable based near the Marble Arch end of Hyde Park, who in 1871 lived in Covent Garden with his wife and nephew Henry Stride, a 3-year-old born in Pimlico, Westminster. However, Henry Alfred Stride's parents were Henry Stride, a law clerk, and Sophia, nee Morgan. Ten years later, in 1881, a Henry Stride is the 12-year-old apprentice to a watchmaker called Robert N. Simpson in Croydon. No known connection to the Strides of Sheerness or Liz Stride.

Although a comedy of errors usually revolves around mistaken and assumed identities, the stories of Mary Malcolm are a tangled skein. They involve a long-lost sister who turned up and saw her weekly for three years. We know Long Liz was very credible and persuasive in court. Maybe Mary Malcolm was conned. The coincidences are quite striking.

Notes

1. International Genealogical Index.
2. *J G Harrod and Co's Postal and Commercial Directory to Dorset and Wiltshire* 1865 edition.
3. Andrew and Malcolm's addresses were in quite a small area. Her Baldwin Gardens 1881 address is very close to Chancery Lane where she claimed to have met her sister. In 1888 she was at 50 Eagle Street, Red Lion Square. This area is close to the law courts of Grey's Inn and also Portpool Lane, where Joseph Barnett stayed with his sister in November 1888 after the death of Mary Kelly. Arthur Machen, the writer, lived in Verulam Buildings in the late 1880s.
4. Witness to the wedding of Andrew and Mary Malcolm, Adolphus Frederick Hatton, according to the 1881 census, was a bookbinder born circa 1817 in Marlborough, Wiltshire, and living at 26 Fetter Lane. Also in the census at Peabody Buildings Lambeth, 9R Block, is one Adolphus Hatton, a 45-year-old vellum book binder. There is a curious overlap here with the life of a previous victim of Jack the Ripper, Mary Ann Nichols, who was born in the area to the south of Chancery Lane, and who at one time lived also in Peabody Buildings, 6D Block, in Lambeth with her husband, who worked in the print trade. A witness to that wedding, Seth Havell, was linked to a famous bookbinding family.
5. Molly Whittington Egan: *Defender of the Insane: Doctor Forbes Winslow*.
6. He was 24 years and 2 months old, a labourer, from the parish of Deal in Kent. He was five foot six-and-a-half inches tall, with fresh complexion, grey eyes, brown hair and no distinguishing marks. He joined the navy at Bromley in Kent on May 23rd 1859. In his career he committed numerous offences, including absence, disobedience and desertion. In 1861, whilst serving on *HMS St George* at Halifax, he deserted and was imprisoned for two years. In 1866 by his own request he was transferred to *HMS Victory*. The captain of the *Victory* queried his record. Eventually he was sent on the

A Tangled Skein?

Megaera to Australia to serve on *HMS Blanche*, from which he eventually deserted in 1872. Attestation for Royal Marines (ATM 157/97/folio 558). "For what Bounty did you enlist(?) Five Pounds and a free kit!"

7 *HMS Victory*, famous since the Battle of Trafalgar, served from 1869 to 1887 as a tender to *HMS Wellington* which had taken over *Victory*'s previous role as stationary flagship of the Commander-in-Chief (*Alan McGowan: HMS Victory: Her Construction, Career and Restoration*, Chatham Publishing, London 1999).

8 W P Gossett: *Lost Ships of the British Navy 1793-1900*.

9 The *Megaera* took him from England to Australia and *HMS Blanche*. In that ship's Record and Establishment Book: 12th October 1871 to 31st December 1872 we find that he was "received from *Megaera*" - JAS SNELLER Deal Kent 26 Mar 35 (ADM 115/108). The *Megaera* became famous for its fatal voyage in 1871. A 1901 book written by the brother of the then captain, Captain Thrupp, deals with the voyage and the ensuing court martial - in which Thrupp's sword was given back to him as he is cleared of blame. George Athelstane Thrupp: *A Short Memoir of Arthur Thomas Thrupp 1828-1889*.

10 The major questions about Sneller concern: 1) His early court-martial. The captain of *HMS Victory* inquired, but it would take a naval historian to make sense of it; 2) His marriage certificate listing him as a widower, whilst his first wife was alive; 3) The fact that after he deserted he came back to England and lived in Portsmouth, a town full of navy officers. He seems to give his name after 1881 to the census takers as John, but both he and his wife Caroline J were born in Deal.

My thanks to Frogg Moody for his encouragement and to both James Marsh and Arthur Conan Doyle for the title.

2010

THOMAS OLIVER WESTON
The Man Who Died Twice and Watched His First Funeral

SUE & ANDY PARLOUR

This article appeared in edition 35 of The Whitechapel Journal

We feature here an intriguing story from the East End about an intriguing man. The story involves many of the names we are familiar with in the Whitechapel murder saga; Dr. Thomas Bond, Coroner Wynne E. Baxter and the Thames Torso mystery. We also witness one of the most bizarre coroner's inquests ever that helped lead to a significant change in the law.

Thomas Oliver Weston died on 30 May 1919. On the previous day he was involved a road accident at the junction of Sidney Street and Oxford Street, in Whitechapel. Sidney Street, in 1911, was the scene of the infamous Siege of Sidney Street involving Russian Anarchists in a shoot-out with the British Army and armed members of the police. Thomas Oliver Weston suffered a terrible death that May Day, being trampled by the hooves of two heavy Suffolk Punch horses, who had bolted after a passing vehicle back-fired. Thomas Oliver Weston died a hero in London's East End and his name will live on forever.

We now go back 104 years, from 2010 to 1906, and 13 years before Thomas was killed.

In 1906, the same Thomas Oliver Weston was officially pronounced dead after a body was pulled from the river Thames at Battersea. A positive identification by his wife, Louisa Weston, and younger brother Walter Henry Weston was made at the mortuary. After the coroner's inquest the body of Thomas Weston was released for burial. His wife and family mourned his passing and using the family's meagre savings gave him a true East End London funeral – a funeral that Thomas Oliver Weston, albeit unknown to his own family, watched! What follows is a true and remarkable story.

Back from the dead

We start this story on the day Thomas Oliver Weston was born, on 28 April 1869 at 3 Fashion Street, Whitechapel. The name entered on his birth certificate was Thomas Oliver Watts, not Weston. As dawn broke on the 28th, Thomas Oliver (Weston) Watts saw daylight. A sickly child, he was not expected to survive. The mortality rate for newborn children in the East End of London at that time was as high as 25%, but survive he did, and six weeks later on 7 June 1869 his birth was registered at the local registry office at Spitalfields. On the birth certificate Elizabeth Watts (his mother) did not exactly tell the truth. For a start, she gave the name of the father as Oliver Watts, when we know it was Oliver Weston! Elizabeth did, however, give the correct occupation of the father as a Sugar Baker. It was to get even more mysterious and suspicious when on 18 July 1869, at Thomas Oliver's baptism in the parish church of St Matthias, Bethnal Green, she gave the name of his father as Samuel Watts. Samuel Watts had been long gone! This name changing was very regular where Elizabeth Watts was concerned. It was most likely for financial gain, as poor people's charities and boards of guardians gave handouts to new mothers and children - two different fathers and names would perhaps mean a double pay out!

Back to Thomas Oliver Weston, who later became a carman. He was not without a few brushes with the law - most seriously when he was arrested in early September 1892 by PC Smith in Gracechurch Street. Thomas Weston was seen driving a cartload of timber down the street, and was continually whipping the two black horses pulling the cart. A crowd surrounded the cart and stopped it. One of the crowd, a Mr. Fenn, asked him why he was being so harsh on the horses, to which Thomas Weston replied "I am obliged to do it or they will stop, and I will not be able to get them going again." Both horses were covered in weals and were lame. It was then that Police Constable Smith stepped in and arrested Weston. He appeared in court the following day and was heavily censured and punished with a fine of £3 with £1 10s costs by Magistrate Alderman Hart, who stated that this was a very bad case of cruelty to two horses quite unfit for work. The fine imposed on Weston by the court was a considerable amount of money in 1892.

It was about this time that Thomas Weston decided he was going to be a wanderer. In order to earn a shilling or two, he would often just go off with a travelling fair or circus, or opt for working on farms, even going to earn money hop-picking in Kent. This he often did without telling any of the family! He could be gone for weeks at a time, leaving Louisa to struggle to keep food on the table and a roof over the children's heads. She did receive money from her wandering husband occasionally, but she mainly relied on handouts from her in-laws and her own family. Thomas would turn up sometimes, but was soon off again. After some of his visits, Louisa was left pregnant! She lost one of her children in childbirth. By 1901, she seems to have had enough, leaving her children with relatives, and went to live in Brighton near her mother-in-law Elizabeth, who in 1891 was with a soldier named William Hacker, and they moved to Brighton soon after he was discharged from the army. William Hacker died in 1899 and Elizabeth had a live-in job with a family at 10 Sterling Place, Hove, and the 1901 census stated she was a widow, another little untruth! Her legal husband, Oliver Weston, in 1901 at the age of 71 was in the Whitechapel Infirmary where he told the staff he was a widower!

Louisa Weston, wife of Thomas, had found a domestic job in 1901 with a family at 20 Port Hall Place, Brighton, and with the job came her own room. She said she was single, although she gave her married name - Weston. Her husband was now living at the Bermondsey Salvation Army Hostel. He stated he was single and working as a labourer at a waste-paper warehouse. Brother Walter Henry Weston was now back from South Africa and was living at 98 Lower Clapton Road, Hackney, East London, with his wife Alice Maud and their four children. Alice Maud suffered two miscarriages but in 1905 gave birth to William Oliver.

It seems by now the Weston family had finally given up on one of their own and disowned Thomas Oliver Weston. His wife, father and brother had not heard anything from him for months, and Louisa had not received any money from her husband to supplement her meagre earnings from taking in laundry or stuffing mattresses with straw. The Weston family now officially reported Thomas to the police as a missing person, giving the police a detailed description including marks or scars. Bearing in mind he had previously been arrested by the police and had been in court, Thomas was already known to the police because he had a criminal record. The only thing the Weston family had heard of Thomas Oliver was the occasional rumour he had been seen in and around the East End.

In mid July 1906, the Weston family heard the news they had feared. The police called at 98 Lower Clapton Road to inform Walter Henry that a body had been pulled from the Thames at Battersea, and from their own records the police believed it to be his missing brother, Bethnal Green labourer Thomas Oliver. The following day Walter and Thomas' wife Louisa journeyed to the Battersea morgue to identify the body. Following is the report from the time:

> *The body was shown to Walter and Louisa. The face of the corpse was in such a condition that the features did not afford facial identification, but there were several peculiarities, which made both the 'widow' and Walter Weston positive that the body was that of Thomas Oliver Weston. In the first place the missing Weston was a very small man under five feet high. The corpse tallied with this measurement and in other physical matters, such as colour of his hair and eyes, but, the strongest evidence of its being Weston was the fact that there was on one of his fingers, a deep depression caused by the wearing of a very tight ring. Weston had such a mark*

on the same finger. He often pawned the ring, so the fact the ring was not on the finger did not affect the identification. Moreover, on the right forearm of the corpse were blurred tattooed letters looking like L.L.N.T., and Weston's right forearm bore the same disfigurement. On the 1st of August the Battersea Coroners Court held an inquest on the death of Thomas Oliver Weston. A verdict of death by accidental drowning was returned. On the evidence of brother Walter and Thomas's wife Louisa his body was released to the family for burial.

Arrangements were made with a local undertaker by the Weston family to bury Thomas Oliver in a style befitting an East Ender. Family and friends clubbed together to give him a good send-off. The body was buried at Bow Cemetery. The funeral was attended by a large crowd. A few days prior to the funeral, Louisa Weston had been given four guineas from the widows fund of the local board of guardians, and also received four guineas from an insurance policy.

When the 'widow' returned home, totally shattered from the events of the day, she was grateful to sit down. However, who should walk in but Thomas Oliver Weston, as hale and hearty as ever! Naturally his wife promptly fainted! Thomas Weston, it appears, had no intention of staying away so long on the day he left home many months earlier, but on hearing of work in the country, and being short of money, had decided to tramp there. He had asked a friend to tell his wife of his plans but his friend had forgotten to give Louisa the message. After Thomas had gone, a corpse supposedly Weston's was found in the river. It has been said that some men have read their own obituaries, but surely very few have lived after being the subject of a coroner's inquest or stood amongst the watching crowd observing his own family burying him!

The police were informed of the apparent 'resurrection' of Thomas, and he was quickly taken into custody. This was another entry on his criminal record, and more was to come. He was kept in a cell until he was called to appear at Battersea Coroner's Court – the same Coroner's Court that had held an inquest into his death on 1 August 1906. So the Westons returned to the coroner's court as they were summoned there by the coroner, Mr. Troutbeck, who was not a happy man. He regarded this whole affair as a slur on his good character, as it was he who sat in charge of the first inquest!

We now refer to one of the many newspaper reports of this very unusual second coroner's inquest, one of the strangest ever held in England:

> *A man who was identified as drowned, and whose body was buried by his relatives, appeared in the Battersea Coroner's Court to explain to the coroner that he really is alive. The man is Thomas Oliver Weston, a labourer, of Bethnal Green. On August the 1st last his wife and brother had positively identified the body of a man, which was recovered from the Thames as his, and buried it. He came home the day of the funeral, and had some difficulty in convincing his relatives that he was alive! When Thomas Oliver Weston entered the witness - box, Mr. Troutbeck, the coroner, said: 'I have sent for you that you might state on oath that you are Thomas Oliver Weston. You know an inquest was held on what was supposed to be your body.' Thomas then swore on oath that he was who he was. The coroner then required him to show certain marks, which his wife and brother had described in identifying the body, the body they had buried. He did so, and then brother Walter Henry Weston was called, he admitted that he had been mistaken in the previous identification. The coroner said that this case illustrated strongly the necessity of freezing apparatus in connection with the mortuaries and of a more scientific system for the identification of bodies.*

The Westons were dismissed and the inquest was closed for the second time.

Interestingly, it was this case that helped to kick-start a system, as Coroner Troutbeck remarked, for preserving bodies longer. This resulted in the 'freezing' of the deceased until the body was officially released for the funeral.

Coroner Troutbeck did have a slight connection to the Jack the Ripper murders some 18 years earlier, when as a Westminster coroner he sat at the inquest on the torso in the Thames mystery, as well as being a confidant of Dr. Thomas Bond.

We finish this first part of the story with a report from the *Nelson Evening Mail* of Rorah, Putanga, New Zealand. Yes, this was by now an International story!

THE DEAD ALIVE –
A CASE OF MISTAKEN IDENTITY

A curious case of mistaken identity recently resulted in the corpse of a man who had been found dead in London's river Thames being buried as that of a person very much alive, and on the day of his own funeral, which he is reported to have observed, later turned up to the great amazement of the witnesses, including his wife and brother who had identified his corpse. Relatives and friends who had attended his funeral were left wondering, if it was not Thomas Oliver Weston they had buried that day, who was it...?

As far as Louisa Weston was concerned, her husband might well have been dead, for soon after the second inquest he was off again! And what did his father Oliver Weston make of it all? He was none too pleased about the whole affair. He had one son who now had a criminal record for beating horses and more minor offences, plus having to hear from his other son, Walter Henry, the sad news that Thomas was dead after he and Louisa had identified him at the Battersea Morgue. The Weston family then buried him, and as we know Thomas was still very much alive, and Thomas had taken great pleasure in watching his own kith and kin bury him and get into debt to do it. To top it all, they had spent all this money on a funeral for a total stranger! Sadly, on 15 April 1907, Oliver Weston died aged 78.

The real death of Thomas Oliver Weston

By 1911, Walter Henry Weston had moved with his family to 30 Eaton Place, Hackney. Now a tram driver, he was supporting his wife and six children, who were living in four rooms. Meanwhile, the one-time widow of Thomas, Louisa Weston, now aged 40, was living at 58 Derbyshire Street, Bethnal Green, with her children Alice 20, Elizabeth 13, Louisa 11, and her son from a previous relationship, Charles, 23. In 1911 Louisa Weston said on the census she was a widow! Well, was she? The answer is no - because husband Thomas Oliver was very much alive and living at the Salvation Army men's home 20 Whitechapel Road. Thomas Oliver Weston, now aged 43, said he was married and a labourer.

The next couple of years rolled by with the occasional visit from Thomas Weston to his family, and sometimes money would arrive for Louisa Weston. The First World War began in August 1914, and the Weston family did their bit. Walter Henry joined up, and because of his service in the Boer War and experience with horses was promoted to full sergeant and posted to the Army Veterinary Corps (AVC). Sgt Weston was mentioned in dispatches for his service in Gallipoli and on the Western Front. His eldest son John (Jack) Oliver Weston was also in the AVC.

November 1914 was the last time all the Weston family were together, as on the 14th Elizabeth Hacker died in Brighton aged 80. Elizabeth had used many names, starting with her maiden name of Veal, then Watts, Weston and finally Hacker. Although registered as Elizabeth Hacker on her death certificate, the only married name she legally ever had was Weston. After the funeral in Brighton the family went their separate ways: Walter and Jack Weston went back to war, as did other members of the family who were related through Elizabeth Hacker, be it as a mother, grandmother, mother-in-law or sister. Daughter Alice Coventry nee Watts and her husband Bill Coventry suffered terrible heartbreak when two of their sons went off to war and never came home.

When the Armistice was finally signed on 11 November 1918, bringing a halt to the carnage of the previous four years, a great feeling of relief swept through the nation. British servicemen, many of who went off to fight as boys, came home as men.

On the bright Friday afternoon of 29 May 1919, Thomas Oliver Weston left the Wildermuth Common Lodging House on Wentworth Street, Whitechapel. Little did he know what fate had in store for him that day, his last on God's Earth. Where was he going? Looking for work? Had he arranged a meeting? We will never know. He crossed the Whitechapel Road and was making his way south down Sidney Street to the junction of Oxford Street, when a vehicle backfired. A horse-drawn beer dray was delivering beer to a pub on the corner of Oxford Street. The loud bang startled the horses, whose draymen were away from the dray. The horses bolted. Ahead in the road was a line of schoolchildren, and heading straight for them were the runaway horses and dray. Thomas Oliver Weston, without one thought for his own safety, ran out in front of the horses, and grabbing the loose reins diverted them away from the children. In doing so Weston was pulled down between the horses, losing his footing and falling to the ground. The heavy hooves trampled on him before he was run over by the steel rimmed wheels of the dray. He had stopped the runaway horses. Thomas averted a terrible tragedy that day and saved the lives of those children, but in doing so gave his own.

Doctors were called from the nearby London Hospital and an ambulance trolley was summoned. A screen was erected around Thomas, whose injuries were very traumatic. He was taken, barely alive, to the hospital where the doctors could not do much for him. His crushed and battered body was beyond help, and within hours he breathed his last while surrounded by his family. Many witnesses came forward to say they had never seen such an act of bravery in their lives, and men who had seen the horrors of war told how Thomas just ran out into the road in front of those runaway horses to grab the reins, with no thought of his own safety, to save those children. This time, unlike in 1906, the family would make no mistake. The mangled body they identified on the 30 May in the morgue of the London Hospital was definitely that of Thomas Oliver Weston. An inquest was called for 2 June and held at the hospital. The verdict of death was given as thus:

> *Violent. Internal haemorrhage, supervening on crushed spleen and kidney and other injuries caused by falling while trying to stop runaway horses (2 horses 4 wheels) when the wheels passed over him. Accidental P.M.*

The coroner was none other than Wynne E. Baxter, a name much familiar to those interested in the unsolved Whitechapel murders of 1888.

The London Hospital

The body of Thomas Oliver Weston was released to the family, who had instructed undertakers James Hawes of 130 Well Street, Hackney, to take care of the funeral arrangements. The Weston family faced a dilemma - they were now having to pay for a second funeral for the same family member. However, donations from the families of those he saved that day helped to cover the costs.

Thomas Oliver Weston, aged 50, was laid to rest in Bow Cemetery with family and friends in attendance, along with many parents of the children he gave his life for on 29 May. We leave this day with these words from his children:

Sleep on dear Father and take thy rest. For God hath done what he thought best. The loss is great that we sustain, but in Heaven we hope to meet again...

Epilogue

You may feel that this is the end of the story, but no! The act of bravery and sacrifice shown by Thomas Weston came to the notice of none other than millionaire, industrialist and philanthropist

Andrew Carnegie. Carnegie was born in 1835 of poor Scottish stock in Dunfermline, Scotland. His family emigrated to America in 1848. With hard work and enterprise being his main principles, Andrew Carnegie became one of the richest men in the world. However, he never forgot his roots and became a benefactor to many important institutions all over the world. In 1908 he established the Carnegie Hero Fund. The aim of the fund, to this day, is to recognise heroism and give financial assistance where necessary to people who have been injured, or to the dependants of those who have been killed in saving and attempting to save another human life or lives. This is a special fund set up by Andrew Carnegie for Great Britain, Ireland, the Channel Islands and the surrounding territorial waters.

Thomas Oliver Weston's name was entered onto the Roll of Heroes & Heroines Book held by the Carnegie Dunfermline and Hero Fund Trustees. His entry states thus:

> *Thomas Weston (51) Wildermouth Lodging House, Wentworth, LONDON, on the 29th May 1919, sustained fatal injuries while attempting to stop a pair of runaway horses at the junction of Sidney Street and Oxford Street, LONDON.*

The Carnegie fund did honour its pledge to give financial assistance to dependants of those killed in acts of bravery. Louisa Weston, now legally a widow, received an allowance of eleven guineas a year from the Carnegie Heroes fund until she died.

Ironically, Andrew Carnegie died in August 1919, only three months after Thomas Oliver Weston.

It was said in the family, with slight irony, that Louisa Weston was much better off financially with husband Thomas dead than ever she was when he was alive! One thing is sure - the name of Thomas Oliver Weston will live on forever in the Carnegie Heroes Fund Book, and in our family.

A TRUE HERO OF THE EAST END

2011

GEORGE HUTCHINSON: WITNESS, SUSPECT OR RED HERRING

IAN PORTER

This article appeared in edition 36 of The Whitechapel Journal

In the following piece the writer, Ian Porter takes a more detailed look at the witness George Hutchinson whose testimony concerning the events leading up to the death of the victim Mary Kelly have been a matter of constant debate throughout the years.

*

George Hutchinson is perhaps the most oft-discussed and controversial of all the witnesses in the Jack the Ripper case. Many tend to concentrate their debate on Hutchinson's detailed description of `gold chain man' and his behaviour in hanging about outside Mary Kelly's place. But I would like to look at what Hutchinson actually did and did not say a little more closely and consider whether the detailed description is the least of our worries about this witness. But whatever one's take on all this is, we always come back to the "yeah but" question of, so why did Abberline believe him? I will consider this too.

Firstly, Hutchinson did not say some of what has come to be attributed to him. Some things have been taken from what the newspapers wrote about him, which was embellished. For example, he is now often quoted as stating that he saw the man the following day in Petticoat Lane. He never said this. It was just press invention. The press also changed his description of the man, making the man sound far darker and more foreign in looks.

Then there is what he did say. It has come to be accepted that Hutchinson had just got back from Romford in Essex. But a pub, still there today as the Pride of Spitalfields, was known locally in those days as the Romford. It's close to Commercial Street where Hutchinson claims he saw Mary with gold chain man. I think it rather more likely Hutchinson said in cockney tones something along the lines of, "I bin dan a Rumford' meaning The Romford pub. He also stated that the man was of Jewish "appearance". The word "appearance" was used in a different context to nowadays. It meant pertaining to clothing, or occasionally to hairstyle, rather than physical features per se. So Hutchinson was stating that the man was dressed like a Jew, rather than necessarily was Jewish. A pedantic point perhaps, but one the researcher has to consider.

I have suspicions about the validity of Hutchinson's statement but its great detail or his odd behaviour are the least of my problems with it. The biggest concern I have is one of geography. Hutchinson stated he chatted with Mary at the corner of Flower & Dean Street, before she headed towards Thrawl Street where the man tapped her on the shoulder, they chatted then walked past him where he remained at Flower & Dean Street. He got a good look at the man because of the light shed from the Queen's Head pub. BUT, the Queen's Head was not on the corner of Flower & Dean Street, it was on the corner off Fashion Street, 120 yards from where he claims he heard the couple speak to each other. And he didn't simply get the names of a pub mixed up - there was no pub on the corner of Flower & Dean Street or any other building that would cast light. Interestingly, Hutchinson's statement, which is still in the public records office, originally stated he was outside the Ten Bells, which is even further away. Someone has at some point crossed out the Ten Bells and written Queen's Head.

Also, this all supposedly occurred on Commercial Street. But the

Spitalfields fruit and veg market was in this street, and it was the early hours at the start of the weekend. The street would have been very busy with horse and carts taking their wares to market. Yet nobody else appears to have seen Mary with gold chain man.

As for Hutchinson's detailed description of the man, his claim to have seen the man brandish a red hankie has often been queried because of the difficulty in seeing colour in the dark under artificial light, but I'm more interested in the gold chain. The only way he could have seen the gold chain the man was wearing on his waistcoat was if the man had his coat open. This means that on a cold, wet November night the man chose to wear his coat open with his gold on display whilst walking past the most notoriously criminal area in London, the Flower & Dean Street rookery, into which even policeman would only venture four at a time. We are asked to believe that this man passed seamlessly through the territory of vicious street gangs and other assorted dodgy characters without his finery changing ownership in a hostile takeover bid. I know Jack was lucky but...

As for his odd behaviour in hanging about for 45 minutes outside Mary's, this is perhaps the least implausible element. IF one believes he did somehow hear and see the couple, and DID see the man's finery in great detail, his hanging about is readily explained by him planning to do what the Flower & Dean Street populace somehow managed not to do, namely relieve the gent of his valuables by mugging him when he came out of Mary's. After all, Hutchinson was jobless at the time and he could have got a tidy sum for the gold chain etc.

So why did Abberline believe him? Well, maybe he did and maybe he didn't. Unfortunately, Abberline's interview notes with Hutchinson have not survived but we do still have Abberline's covering report. In it he says he "interrogated' Hutchinson. The use of this word rather than "interviewed' suggests Abberline originally suspected Hutchinson of telling lies. He also had Hutchinson go to identify the body. But Mary's ex-boyfriend Joe Barnett and her landlord John McCarthy had already formally identified her, so one wonders if Abberline did this just to see Hutchinson's reaction when he saw the appalling mutilations?

One also has to consider the pressure Abberline was under. Could he afford to ignore an eye witness claiming to have got such a great sighting of the man? If he had, he could imagine the head-lines in the papers - ABBERLINE IGNORES EYE-WITNESS. Also, the police were concerned about the level of anti-Semitism at the time and fearful of vigilantism. Consider how they washed away the Goulston Street graffiti even before they took a photo of it. If they were seen to be ignoring an eye witness who said the killer was of "Jewish appearance", who knows what might happen. As for Hutchinson not coming forward for three days - he probably explained that away to Abberline by saying he had been away looking for work over the weekend, and he didn't hear about the murder until he got back, which would have been plausible enough.

So why would Hutchinson lie? Another eye witness, a well respected sober woman, stated categorically that she saw and spoke to Mary the day after she was supposed to have been killed. Yet she was pretty much ignored, and was warned off at the inquest for wasting the court's time. And the whole Ripper enquiry is full of statements and witness accounts that simply don't seem to add up or cross reference with each other. These people had lived very simple lives, but suddenly they're at the centre of the world's press, having police, newspapermen, inquest barristers, you name it, asking them questions. Some appear to have had a desire for recognition; a brief moment of glory in their drab lives.

Did Hutchinson invent the Jewish gent suspect because he was fearful he had been seen in the vicinity at the time of the murder, and the killer being such a gent was one of the rumours doing the rounds at the time? Some have gone as far to suggest Hutchinson was Jack the Ripper or a lookout for the killer, but I would argue it is more likely a simple man's imagination running wild out of fear he had been seen in the area, or he was just like so many other witnesses, a man looking for reflected glory. He talked himself into being a suspect for a while, just as that man in Portugal did in the Maddie McCann case, and just as D'Onston Stephenson (Dr. D) did in

George Hutchinson: Witness, Suspect or Red Herring

"I COULD SWEAR TO THE MAN ANYWHERE"
HUTCHINSON.

the Jack the Ripper case.

Hutchinson's statement fits the middle class gent profile so well, that it appears to have been given more credence in the last 40 years, in the Gull/Sickert/Maybrick era, than it ever was in 1888.

2012

WATT DO YOU THINK THE TRUE IDENTITY OF JACK THE RIPPER WAS?

Documenting the Whitechapel Murders and 1970s British Television

ANDREW O'DAY

This article appeared in edition 46 of The Whitechapel Journal

The 1973 BBC *Jack the Ripper* begins with all the hallmarks of a Ripper production. It is nighttime. The first close-up shot of a flame is replaced by a shot of a gas lamp; the sound of an unseen horse trotting along the cobbled streets dominates the soundtrack; an unfortunate woman walks down an alleyway followed by a man, casting shadows on the brick wall; she turns around; there is a close-up of her looking upwards followed by one of her mouth as she screams.

However, that sequence, which occurs in less than a minute, and other brief filmed inserts mostly in the pre-credit sequences to the episodes, are where the similarities end. Rather the serial (written by Elwyn Jones and John Lloyd, produced by Paul Bonner and Leonard Lewis, and broadcast from July 12 to August 17 1973), set in the studio, sees Detective Chief Superintendent Barlow (Stratford Johns) and Detective Chief Inspector Watt (Frank Windsor) sifting through documents in an effort to succeed where the police of 1888 failed and uncover the true identity of 'Jack the Ripper'. The serial shifts between the late 20th century and speakers from the 19th.

Before delving into the documentary elements of the production, it is important to note other techniques for drawing in viewers. It has been observed that "*Z Cars* became something of a brand for the BBC" ('The Works of Troy Kennedy Martin - Screenwriter') and among the original characters from 1962 were Barlow and Watt. In 1966, Barlow and Watt were given their own spin-off, *Softly, Softly*, remaining in it until 1969, while Barlow then went on to his own series *Barlow at Large* (1971-75). *Jack the Ripper*'s success is illustrated by the fact that Barlow and Watt went on to appear in 1977's six-part series *Second Verdict* which repeated the formula of the pair working on unsolved mysteries from the past, or on miscarriages of justice.

The opening titles of the 1973 *Jack the Ripper* explicitly refer to the serial as a 'Documentary investigation'. Derek Paget reveals that the word documentary etymologically derives from the word 'documents'. Paget points out that 'The first recorded usages of the adjective 'documentary' in English are from the early nineteenth century and can be linked to a post-Enlightenment faith in... rationality' but that the 'word developed from a much earlier noun, 'document', that had been in use from around 1400 and that is clearly connected to the invention of the printing press and the resultant production of paper records of events and transactions'. 'Importantly', Paget continues, 'these words are connected from the earliest times with 'evidence' and the 'evidential' (p.144). Paget writes that 'Use of documentary material is an important and distinctive convention of' films that blend fact and drama (p.105).

Indeed, in the 1973 *Jack the Ripper*, Barlow and Watt conduct their investigation based on books, papers, and newspaper articles which they are explicitly shown reading. There are cuts between Barlow and Watt looking at their sources and scenes from the 1888 inquests, scenes from newspaper offices of copy being recited; and scenes of people supplying theories as to the identity of the Ripper. This gives the impression that these scenes are records being acted out for us. The 19th century scenes are integrated with the 20th century ones with occasionally Barlow and Watt speaking over the inserts, Barlow commenting that one man is a fool, and Barlow stating to Watt 'What are you on about now' after a speaker has given information.

Most of the Barlow and Watt 20th century scenes are set in one room, with the exception of the very brief filmed location shooting at the beginning of the final episode where the pair visit a couple of the murder sites as they appeared in the 1970s, as all they have need of is documents. Tellingly, the only other time in all six episodes where a character leaves this room is when Barlow exits to get hold of confidential files, his journey not seen.

Paget has noted that 'The use of witnesses' gives a sense 'of someone providing 'authenticating detail' in relation to an event' (p.276) but, of course, in the case of the Whitechapel Murders so much of the testimony was conflicting. The documents do not tell them who the Ripper was and it is significant that many of the documents have been removed.

Paget further reveals how the camera can fix moments and bring them into the future (p.122-23). He writes that one 'major premise upon which the supremacy of the camera is built is that it will give us access to external events which otherwise would be lost except through the very different agency of report' (p.124). The idea of the camera and report is crucial to the Jack the Ripper case and is highlighted in productions such as this one. We are told that Sir Charles Warren ordered the writing on the wall in Goulston Street, 'The Juwes are the Men That Will Not be blamed for Nothing', to be wiped before a picture could be taken, giving as his reason that the writing would lead to anti-Semitism. However, a police officer copied the writing down exactly meaning that Barlow is able to reproduce it precisely on a blackboard. The actual writing on the wall is reproduced in productions like Wickes' 1988 mini-series, where there is also the (incorrect) idea that a photograph be taken of Mary Jane Kelly's eyes as it was said that the eyes capture the last thing that they see. But even had the writing on the wall been photographed we would still be left with the mystery of whether, based on the spelling Juwes, the Ripper was a Freemason. Also while photographs of some suspects are shown in the 1973 production there is no solid evidence linking them to the murders.

Paget also refers to the incorporation of newsreel in such dramas, designed to provide a sense of authenticity. He writes that these dramas 'are much more likely to incorporate...news images and devices. The presence of documentary material is in some ways a badge of quality' (p.111). The newsreel exteriors could, remarks Paget, be mixed with studio set interiors (p.199), although this is not the case in the *Jack the Ripper* serial. In the final episode, Watt gives Barlow a roll of tape which Barlow holds up to examine. There is then an immediate cut to a screen with the real Joseph Sickert (in the late 20th century) providing the theory of Queen Victoria's grandson Prince Eddie having married the lower class Catholic woman Annie Crook and having sired a child by her and of the prostitutes having been murdered as a result.

Furthermore, the sense is given of the production as being a documentary investigation by the fact that as in real life it does not provide closure, it does not provide an answer as to who the Ripper was. While countless Ripperologists have sought the true identity of 'Jack the Ripper', the Whitechapel Murderer's very facelessness is crucial to the way in which he has been seized upon and represented in other film and television productions. In their introduction to the edited volume *Jack the Ripper: Media, Culture, History*, Alexandra Warwick and Martin Willis argue that this facelessness left a blank space which could only be filled by the imagination. The case of the Whitechapel Murderer therefore blurs the boundaries between the known and the unknown, and between reality and fiction. Fiction is a product of the imagination, the filling in of a blank space. So, while the Whitechapel Murderer is a historical figure (we know that he really existed and perpetrated the murders of some prostitutes), he is also a nebulous figure, who continually evaded detection and who, especially today, cannot be pinned down. There thus exists epistemological uncertainty. Later films such as *Murder by Decree*

(1979) and *From Hell* (2001), and a television production like David Wickes' 1988 centennial mini-series *Jack the Ripper* offer solutions as to who the Ripper was. In the films, the murderer was Sir William Gull acting on orders from the British government to silence a group of prostitutes who were aware of the secret marriage between Prince Eddie and Annie Crook. In Wickes' mini-series, the killer was also Gull, again accompanied by coach driver John Netley, although his motivation was that he was trying to understand the Jekyll and Hyde nature of his own mind. In the 1973 serial, Barlow and Watt bounce different theories off one another, but do not settle on any particular one. The serial ends with Barlow stating that the authorities of the day did get near to Jack the Ripper; that Sir Melville Macnaghten named three suspects in the official file who could not answer back (either dead or incarcerated in a mental asylum) to stop busybodies poking around; and that while he and Watt have been going around in circles the Director of Public Prosecutions has known all along the identity of the killer. 'Only he isn't telling', Barlow concludes.

I'd like to turn to concentrate on the style of the production. On a blog (*Vintage British TV*), a writer notes that 'this is very definitely old style television. Action sequences are virtually non-existent and the script must be one of the wordiest I've encountered'. Leah Panos writes that 'throughout the 1970s the television studio remained the predominant site for television drama'. While this is a generalization, Panos explains that 'theatre had exerted a strong influence over television drama's forms and practices, as well as audience expectations of the medium, and although this began to be challenged in the mid-1960s with technological advances and institutional shifts, theatrical forms of drama remained prevalent' (p.274). Panos argues that television which concentrated on words was the writer's medium as opposed to the director's (p.274). Madeline MacMurraugh-Kavanagh and Stephen Lacey, discussing Play for Today, argue that 'film was regularly used by only a small group of producers and directors' like Tony Garnett and Ken Loach, and that 'Studio-bound production…always remained in the ascendant in terms of sheer bulk of plays produced, and this

Watt Do You Think The True Identity of Jack the Ripper Was?

Frank Windsor as DCS Watt in 1973's Jack the Ripper
Courtesy David Wickes

remained the case until the 1980s' (p.59). Evidently the studio bound nature of most of the *Jack the Ripper* serial tied in both with its concentration on documents and with television practices of its day.

In terms of being wordy, the 1973 *Jack the Ripper* provides variety through the use of different tones. For example, there are moments of comedy when Barlow refers to the lunacy of some of the authorities of the day. There are a range of colourful characters such as a male prostitute giving evidence connected with the Cleveland Street scandal, linked to the Ripper case. Additionally, at the end of the third episode, a lengthy and poignant speech is given about Mary Jane Kelly's funeral and rather than then cutting directly into a comment by Barlow or Watt there is silence in their room continuing the somber mood. The fact that the serial runs without an incidental music score adds to the documentary feeling.

However, the director's role in realizing this production is important. The serial had 3 directors, directing 2 episodes each: Leonard Lewis (epis. 1 and 4), Gilchrist Calder (epis. 2 and 5), and David Wickes (epis. 3 and 6). The direction of the Barlow and Watt scenes is notable and provides variety for scenes set in one room and recorded in the studio: for example, at the end of the third episode Watt challenges Barlow to get access to the private files and after Barlow has asked whether Watt is 'challenging' him Watt gets up and faces Barlow with there being a close-up of each of them. At the very end of the serial, Barlow tells Watt that someone knows the identity of the murderer 'Only they're not telling', and there is a quick zoom-in to a close-up of Barlow for dramatic effect.

The two timezones are also integrated visually, using the studio settings, creating a sense of unity for the viewer. At one point in the third episode, a woman, declaring that the sight of a victim is one she shall carry to her grave, puts a drink to her mouth and at that very moment there is a cut to Watt taking a drink away from his mouth. Later in that same episode, there is a shot of a jury member sitting in court, immediately followed by one of Barlow rising. Moreover, the 20th century setting and the 19th century setting are linked in the first episode, when it is stated that the police were going round in circles trying to keep up with the case. At this point, there is a cut from Barlow and Watt to the interior of the 19th century police station with Inspector Abberline sat at the head of a table. Noticeably the scene begins with the police officers moving around the table in a circular fashion, thereby mirroring the statement. Also interesting is the way at the very end of the serial Barlow says that he and Watt have been going round in circles while someone knows the identity of the killer, mirroring the 19th century police from earlier.

I'd like to now examine the camerawork and the use of sets and props in the *Jack the Ripper* serial further. Thus far, I've shown how the serial is a 'Documentary Investigation' and significantly the camera frequently moves gradually in closer and closer on the talking subject in an investigative manner. This is the case of witnesses at the different inquests to the murders, or a character giving the police a description of the murderer, or a woman telling the story, or different people giving their theories not only to those around them but also to us. There is a shot, for instance, of Macnaghten telling a couple of people his theories but a close-up of him shows him not only looking in their direction but also directly to the camera. Again the fact that this is a 'Documentary Investigation' works in tandem with the practices of television. Paget writes that television, with its small screen, 'is pre-eminently a drama of faces and eyes' (p.39). The exception in the serial is Queen Victoria writing letters at her desk; a voice-over is used and close-ups are not employed.

On top of all this, the production does give the sense of the social history of the day. The fact that there was a class division is not only emphasized by different accents but also through some of the lavish surroundings of key officials (e.g. leather chairs, ornaments, plants) and their smoking cigars. In the first episode, Mrs. Barnett, known for her good works along with her husband, speaks in a smooth voice, and says that her husband has spoken at Oxford and elsewhere. She speaks of the way in which the poor of Whitechapel cannot afford tea, yet at that point there is a shot of her carefully pouring herself a cup.

Paget argues that 'docudrama is effectively the term of choice for discussion of' 'his subject' and notes that 'all attempts to standardize definitions' such as of 'drama documentary' and 'documentary drama' are 'doomed' (p.15). Journalistic commentary routinely mixes the terms 'dramadoc' and 'docudrama' (p.15). Paget does draw a distinction, however between 'docudrama' and a series like *NYPD Blue*, which is 'intended to convey broad truths about something of social importance', stating that 'To be a docudrama is to be altogether closer to documents - to factual templates' (p.16). But Paget highlights that documentary style is often just as important (p.155). Also, the two terms, 'drama documentary' and 'documentary drama' are useful to a degree in helping us realize that there are some distinctions between the 1973 *Jack the Ripper* and Wickes' 1988 mini-series and I'd like to conclude by examining these. Paget writes that 'In performance a drama-documentary will tend to use the names and identities of real historical individuals, and its plot will stay close to the pattern of (relatively) verifiable real-events...A documentary drama, on the other hand, will tend to use fictional constructs, such as an invented plot and characters composited from several real-life originals' (p.156). In the 1980s, British playwright and essayist David Edgar wrote that 'In drama-documentary, our interest is in the rights and wrongs of what is being represented...or the credibility of the argument...In documentary drama, on the other hand, the doc is merely a means to the dram' (Paget p.167). Although the 1988 mini-series uses (mostly) real-life figures, it is in many ways fabricated and to use Edgar's phrase, 'the doc is' largely 'a means to the dram'. Credibility was provided, however, in the 1973 production through the Ripper's identity not being given closure, although the characters of Barlow and Watt are fictional. There are problems with the distinctions made here; for example, the BBC's 1960s play *Cathy Come Home*, frequently labeled a 'documentary drama' and produced within a drama department, was designed to get the audience to think about social issues (Paget pp.209-12).

Finally, Paget notes that 'Docudramas require pre-production research and this is a key marker of difference between docudrama and other kinds of drama...Docudrama makers habitually describe their research in adjectives signifying conscientiousness. Research is never other than 'detailed', 'extensive', 'painstaking...' (p.23, p.25). Sue Davies acted as researcher for the 1988 mini-series and indeed she recorded the Special Edition DVD commentary with Wickes; and a narrative voice from outside the drama refers to 'extensive' and 'painstaking' research having been conducted as the words scroll up a black screen. Although these features are not present in the 1973 serial, it has evidently been meticulously researched and deals with how documents are read from the present and is less fictionalized.

References

Author unknown, '*Jack the Ripper* (BBC) 1973', 23 March 2007, vintagebrittv.blogspot.co.uk/2007/03/jack-ripper-bbc-1973.html (accessed 31 July 2012).

Madeleine MacMurraugh-Kavanagh and Stephen Lacey, 'Who Framed Theatre?: The 'Moment of Change' in British TV Drama, *New Theatre Quarterly* 15 (1999), 58-74.

Derek Paget, *No Other Way To Tell It: Docudrama on Film and Television*. 2nd edition. Manchester, Manchester University Press, 2011.

Leah Panos, 'Realism and Politics in Alienated Space: Trevor Griffith's Plays of the 1970s in the Television Studio', *New Theatre Quarterly* 26 (2010), 273-286.

Alexandra Warwick and Martin Willis, eds, *Jack the Ripper: Media Culture, History*. Manchester, Manchester University Press, 2007.

'The Works of Troy Kennedy Martin – Screenwriter'. www.news.bbc.co.uk/dna/place-lancashire/plain/A17526008 (accessed 31 July 2012).

I'd like to thank Professor Jonathan Bignell for suggesting some secondary sources for this article and to those 'gods' whose names must not be uttered who made a copy of the serial available.

2013

THE DIARY OF JACK THE RIPPER: 20 YEARS ON

ROBERT SMITH

The following article was first published in October 2013 in edition 52 of The Whitechapel Journal, and revised in January 2016

I was initially reluctant to accept Frogg Moody's invitation to write an article for the Whitechapel Journal to mark the 20th anniversary of the publication of *The Diary of Jack the Ripper* by Shirley Harrison, which was published by my company, Smith Gryphon Limited, in October 1993. Did I really want to say anything more about a document, which many Ripper-interested people continue to dismiss as a modern hoax?

Then he said something that caught my interest: "No-one has ever proved the Diary to be a fake." And, of course, he is right. By contrast, consider the infamous handwritten forgeries produced in the 40 years before the Diary was published. In 1957, Amalia and Rosa Panvini were speedily exposed as the authors of thirty volumes of what they claimed to be Mussolini's diaries. Similarly, the German Federal Archives took just two days to prove on 6th May 1983, that Konrad Kujau had forged the Hitler diaries, and had written them on paper manufactured after WWII. Kujau was arrested eight days later.

If the Diary is of recent composition, why is there still no solid evidence that a forgery has been perpetrated? It is almost 25 years since I acquired the publishing rights in 1992 from literary agent, Doreen Montgomery at Rupert Crew Limited, representing Michael Barrett, a former scrap metal dealer and the Diary's owner at that time. If the Diary is of recent composition, why is there still no solid evidence that a forgery has been committed? Why has not one witness ever come forward during this whole period with verifiable evidence of who wrote the Diary and when it was produced. My primary objective in this article is to establish that the Diary is, in fact, a genuine Victorian document probably written in 1888/89.

Attempts at Hoax-busting

Tests and examinations conducted by more than 30 experts on the Diary's ink and paper overwhelmingly point to it being written in the late 19th Century. However, some were not convinced that it is that old. One such was Kenneth Rendell, renowned for exposing the fake Hitler diaries. He was commissioned by the American publishers, Time Warner, to examine the Diary and submit a report. The publishers had bought USA rights in *The Diary of Jack the Ripper* from me, but were spooked by negative headlines appearing in *The Washington Post* and wanted out. I personally brought the Diary to Rendell and his team of experts in Chicago in August 1993 (below). Although, in his opinion, the Diary was a forgery, he provided no

The Rendell team examining the Maybrick Diary in Chicago in August 1993: Kenneth Rendell (left), Maureen Casey Owens and Robert Kuranz. Copyright Robert Smith 1993

scientific evidence to support this assertion. On the contrary, he expressly commended and accepted the extensive forensic testing of the Diary ink, which Shirley Harrison had commissioned from Dr. Nicholas Eastaugh in 1992. Dr. Eastaugh had favourably concluded that the ink was "not inconsistent with a date of 1888". Even more extraordinary, Rendell reported the results of an ion migration test commissioned by him, which dated the Diary as being written in "1921 plus or minus 12 years", i.e. as early as 1909. While not endorsing the Diary as Victorian, he had *de facto* conceded that it could be a forgery of Edwardian origin.

Self-styled hoax-buster, Melvin Harris, also set out to discredit the Diary's authenticity. Although the physical diary is certainly a black leather and clothbound Victorian scrapbook, he was determined to convince the media, that the Diary's author had used a black manuscript ink, manufactured by Diamine Limited in Liverpool, which contains a modern preservative called chloroacetamide. The proposal originated with *Liverpool Daily Post* reporter, Harold Brough, who had been advised by the Art Shop in School Lane, that this ink would be appropriate for someone wanting to imitate a Victorian manuscript ink. So, in October 1994, Harris commissioned a test on two "full stops" of the Diary ink from Dr. Diana Simpson of Analysis For Industry. Her report to him stated: "...chloroacetamide was indicated to be present in the ink used"; but, shockingly, in a letter to me of 31st July 2003, Dr. Simpson confirmed that Harris had only asked AFI "to analyse for its presence or absence without quantification". I had been astonished to read in her slightly earlier letter, dated 29th April 2003, that she had found only "6.5 parts per million" or, in percentage terms, 0.00065% of chloroacetamide in the dry Diary ink. That miniscule amount, no more than a trace, was undoubtedly caused by cross-contamination during the testing process. In stark contrast, Diamine's Chief Chemist, Dr. Alec Voller, confirmed by letter that chloroacetamide accounted for a whacking 3.28% of the chemical ingredients listed in Diamine's formula for its black manuscript ink in dry form, i.e. more than 5000 times the amount of chloroacetamide reported by Dr. Simpson. In the following year, the Department of Colour Chemistry and Dyeing at the University of Leeds performed further tests on the Diary ink and unequivocally confirmed, that there was no chloroacetamide at all in the ink, thereby ruling out the possibility that Diamine ink had been used to write the Diary.

Another attempt to undermine the Diary's credibility centred on the colour of the ink. It was set off by an informal comment made in 1998 by author and academic, Martin Fido, who remembered the ink looking "too blue", when he had viewed the Diary five years earlier. How could this be? I have examined the Diary many dozens of times over the last 21 years, and, during that time, the colour of the ink has remained constantly "generally dark grey in colour", as described by forensic document examiner, Dr. David Baxendale, in his 1992 report commissioned by Shirley Harrison. Dr. Voller hammered the point home, when examining the Diary in my King's Cross offices in October 1995: "...a manuscript ink has a black tracer and is black to start with, whereas a registrar's ink is blue to start with and turns black with age. This [the Diary ink] never has been a blue ink, it was black from the very beginning." So, it simply was not possible for it ever to have looked blue.

I finally found the evidence I needed to settle once and for all both the chloroacetamide and the ink colour issues. In mid-2012, I obtained one of two sealed bottles of Diamine Black Manuscript Ink from Shirley Harrison, supplied to her in 1996 by Dr. Voller. Following a procedure proposed by him, I was able to demonstrate to the audience attending the 2012 Ripper conference in York, that the Diamine ink, when applied on a variety of Victorian papers with a steel-nibbed dipping pen, is not dark grey like the Diary ink, but very definitely black. I held up several representative pages from the Diary and asked the members of the audience to compare the colour of the ink on those pages with the colour on the various Victorian papers. They all agreed, including Martin Fido, who was present, that the Diamine ink samples were unquestionably far blacker and denser than the dark grey ink of the Diary. After the conference, Martin generously offered his revised opinion to me in an email:

"I thought you proved beyond doubt that the ink was not Diamine (something I've been getting my scientist students to see for some years, as I show Alec Voller's opinions and the number of elements found, that don't match)."

In short, the ink-based challenges had failed, and Dr. Eastaugh's original conclusion in 1992, that the Diary ink was "not inconsistent with a date of 1888", had been well and truly sustained.

A Year of Confessions

1994 was a critical year for the Diary and for Michael Barrett and his former wife, Anne. On 2nd January, following a violent domestic episode, Anne left the marital home in Goldie Street, Anfield, taking Caroline, their 13 year-old daughter with her. The Diary became a potent weapon in their bitter feud played out during that year. Michael was aware by May 1994, that Paul Feldman was intent on establishing that the Diary had been in Anne's family for generations. His company, Duocrave Limited, had acquired the video and film rights in the Diary from Smith Gryphon in December 1992. He had made a TV and video documentary in 1993, presented by Michael Winner, and was now in the process of selling the movie rights to New Line Cinema in L.A. Feldman was coming increasingly under pressure from the studio to provide proof of the Diary's ownership. Destabilised by alcohol and the threat of Anne claiming the publishing rights in the Diary for herself, Michael flipped and retaliated with a rage-inspired "confession" that he had forged it. This revelation was reported in the *Liverpool Daily Post* on Saturday 25th June 1994, but retracted by his solicitors two days later. Michael has never managed to produce a single document or any other verifiable evidence in support of his confession. As he has since explained, his summer of madness was fuelled by his desire "to get back at Anne". It was now Anne's turn to retaliate, by immediately instigating divorce proceedings.

Then, just a month or so after Michael's "confession", Anne fired off a sensational revelation of her own. She had recorded a tape in Liverpool on Sunday 31st July 1994 for Paul Feldman, which he played back to Doreen Montgomery, Shirley Harrison and me in his Baker Street offices a few days later. In stunned silence, we listened to the voice of Anne, claiming that she had first seen the Diary in her father's house in 1968-69. 80-year-old Billy Graham, very ill with a heart condition and an inoperable tumour, backed up his daughter's story, describing how his stepmother, Edith Formby, had given the Diary to him at Christmas 1950. The story went, that Edith Formby's mother had been given it by a friend, who had been a servant in the Maybrick household. Whilst it could have happened that way, Anne could offer no evidence to support her claims, and her father died of a heart attack just three months later on 12th November. It may just have been a fortuitous coincidence, that Anne's account of her father inheriting the Diary came on cue to satisfy the ownership concerns of New Line Cinema, who, after months of negotiations with Feldman, finally signed the "Acquisition Agreement" on 23rd August 1994. The film has still not been made.

Michael has never deviated from the story that the Diary was given to him in 1991 by retired newspaper compositor, Tony Devereux, a drinking mate of Michael's from his local pub, The Saddle in Fountains Road, Anfield. According to Michael, Devereux refused to divulge how he came by it. With another twist of the knife, Anne stated on the tape, that it was she, who had given the Diary to Devereux, making him promise not to tell Michael about her role. Neither account could be checked with Devereux himself, as he had died in August 1991. I could not believe any of Anne's revelations. Why wouldn't she, as a co-beneficiary of the book's royalties, have spoken about the Diary's origins, if true, to Michael and ourselves two years earlier, so providing much needed and timely provenance for the Diary at its publication?

For his part, Michael, who has been completely sober for many years, consistently holds firmly to his belief that the Diary is "genuine" and was written by James Maybrick. Such was the extraordinary strength of his conviction that, in order to protect the Diary and ensure that his and Shirley Harrison's book would be published by my company in October 1993 as planned, he rejected a staggering £15,000 offer in March 1993 to sell the Diary. The formal offer was made covertly through Paul Feldman's solicitors. Feldman's audacious plan was to ambush the publishing and all other rights in the Diary, and to write the book himself. To bring an immediate and permanent stop to his scheme, Michael and Anne agreed to transfer their ownership of the Diary to my company for a nominal one pound. In consultation with their literary agent, I drew up an agreement to that effect, which they both signed on 23rd March 1993. With Michael's continuing blessing, I remain the Diary's owner and custodian to this day.

The Diary and Battlecrease House

At the beginning of 1994, we still didn't have a satisfactory explanation for how and where the Diary first surfaced in 1992. The obvious place to look was Battlecrease House, James Maybrick's impressive home in leafy Aigburth on the outskirts of Liverpool, where he had died from arsenic or strychnine poisoning on 11th May 1889. At first, Paul Feldman believed that one or more of the electricians employed by the Liverpool firm of Portus and Rhodes, who had worked in the house in early 1992, were involved in the Diary's removal. He set out with vigour to prove his suspicions and to extract confessions from them. Then, around May 1994, he suddenly changed tack and instigated the campaign that led to Anne and her father claiming that the Diary had been passed down to them via her father's Granny Formby.

However, I became convinced that Michael was personally connected to one of the electricians, who had worked at Battlecrease in early 1992. On Saturday 26th June 1993, during one of my many visits to Liverpool, I persuaded Michael to introduce me to this electrician at The Saddle in Fountains Road, the road where, significantly, the electrician was living. He told me, that he had found "a book" under the floorboards at Battlecrease, and had "thrown it into a skip". He added that he didn't know what the book was.

In May 1997, I unexpectedly received an independent tip-off about the involvement of the Portus and Rhodes electricians from a colleague, London lawyer, Stephen Shotnes. He had coincidentally been in Liverpool seeing a client on a totally unrelated matter. When their business was completed, they went for a drink and the client started to chat about what he knew of the Diary story. Hearing about their conversation on Stephen's return to London, we decided to go back to Liverpool with a tape recorder. I don't have the space here to go into the details of our many interviews with Stephen's client and the people he led us to, but I can affirm that their statements, when pieced together, strongly indicated to me that one of the electricians, who had worked at Battlecrease in early 1992, had taken the Diary from under the floorboards on the first floor, while fitting night storage heaters, including in the room that had been James Maybrick's bedroom (shown below), where he had died.

The word in Liverpool was that a scrap metal dealer had bought the Diary for £25 "in a pub in Anfield". I don't, in fact, believe that the electrician, whom I met at The Saddle, actually took the Diary from Battlecrease, but I am certain that it was he, who gave or sold the Diary to Michael Barrett, just prior to Michael's first phone call about it to Rupert Crew Limited on 9th March 1992. Further confirmation was to come from the respected historical crime researcher, Keith

Robert Smith outside Battlecrease House. James Maybrick's bedroom, where the Diary was very probably discovered in early 1992, was on the first floor above the bay window

Skinner, who conducted later investigations, and had this to say, somewhat enigmatically, to those in Liverpool attending The Trial of James Maybrick in May 2007:

> *If I was free to disclose all the information and evidence in my possession, I would have no doubt that, if placed before a jury, they would have no choice but to conclude that the Diary had come out of Battlcrease.*

A Trio of Red Herrings

I will now briefly look at three of the most persistent objections to the text of the Diary being written by James Maybrick (or a member of the Maybrick family).

How did a brief five word quotation ("Oh, costly intercourse of death") from a poem, *Sancta Maria Dolorum*, by 17th Century religious poet, Richard Crashaw, find its way into the Diary manuscript? Diary sceptics insisted that it was impossible for James Maybrick to have known Crashaw's poetry. Shirley Harrison had asked Michael Barrett to go to the English literature reference section of Liverpool Central Library and try to track down the source of the quotation. On the afternoon of 30th September 1994, an excited Michael Barrett rang Paul Feldman's secretary to announce that he had just found the elusive quotation in the Library. The five words begin a four-line quotation from Crashaw's poem, which was reproduced on page 184 of the hardback edition of *Sphere History of Literature Volume 2*, published by Sphere in 1986. But, within days, Michael had returned to the summer madness of his late June "confession", insisting that he himself had inserted the quotation in the Diary. He claimed that he had found it in a copy of the Sphere book, which the publishers had donated to him for a charity event in 1989. As Sphere had first published the edition only three years previously, Michael's copy would have been in near mint condition, if indeed he really had owned one prior to his finding the quotation in the Library.

Melvin Harris leapt on Michael's discovery of the quotation as proof positive that he must have forged the Diary. However, reminiscent of his gross deception regarding Diamine ink, Harris claimed that Michael's copy had a "binding fault", causing it to fall open naturally at the said quotation, so presenting itself to Michael to be popped into the Diary. In reality, there was no "binding fault" in the edition. I have bought and examined several copies of the Sphere book in mint condition from the same original 1986 impression, and can categorically confirm that all the copies were printed and bound perfectly. Not one of them falls open at page 184, or at any other page for that matter. While it is true that Michael did own a hardback copy of the Sphere book, far from looking new, it is battered and jacketless. When I questioned Michael about his copy in a telephone conversation on 19th December 2006, he admitted to me that he had bought it in a second-hand bookshop in Central Liverpool "a day or two" *after* his discovery of the quotation in the library.

So, could James Maybrick have been familiar with Crashaw's poetry? Very easily, as his poems were readily available to Victorian readers. This particular quotation was prominently displayed in the top line of page 187 of *The Complete Works of Richard Crashaw*, a popular edition published in 1858 by John Russell Smith of Soho Square, London. It must have been a sizable printing, as I have bought no less than five copies of this edition in recent years, when browsing in various second-hand bookshops along Charing Cross Road, London. Another edition of Crashaw's complete works was published in 1866, in London, Edinburgh, and in Liverpool itself by G. Philip and Son, when James Maybrick would have been 28. Interestingly, the publishers' offices and retail shop were in Liverpool's main shopping street, at 20 Church Street, just around the corner from the Maybrick family home in Church Alley, and almost next to Liverpool's Anglican Pro-Cathedral, St Peter's, where both Maybrick's father and grandfather had been the Parish Clerk. So it was not at all "impossible" that a well-educated middle-class cotton merchant with strong family connections with the Parish Church of Liverpool, would know those memorable words by the religious poet, perhaps from a copy of Crashaw's poetry purchased from G. Philip and Son in Church Street.

A second contentious issue is that the handwriting of James Maybrick's will made on 25th April 1889, just a fortnight prior to his death on 11th May, does not obviously match the writing in the Diary. But did James Maybrick himself write the will or was it his brother, Michael, or a lawyer? It twice misspells his daughter, Gladys's second name (Eveleyn instead of Evelyn), an odd mistake for a father to make. Forensic document examiner, Sue Iremonger, has noted the resemblance of James's handwriting to that of Michael Maybrick. Whoever wrote the Diary, there is no evidence to prove that the handwriting is other than late 19th Century. I have many examples of writing from that period in a similar style. In any event, a person's handwriting can vary dramatically, either intentionally to deceive, or subconsciously as a result of being emotionally or mentally stressed.

If the Diary had been written as recently as 1992, its author should have been quickly identified. We had been able to eliminate each of the three most likely suspects, Michael Barrett, Anne Barrett and Tony Devereux, for a whole host of substantial reasons, not least, there being no similarities between their handwritings and the Diary, but also the thorough investigation in Liverpool of the Barretts (and their computer files) by two Scotland Yard detectives in 1993. No other plausible candidates have so far emerged. It is reasonable to conclude that, if we accept the Diary ink and the handwriting style as being Victorian, then so is the writer.

The third issue around James Maybrick, which exercised the Diary sceptics, is the reference to the writer taking "refreshment at the Poste House". It is true that there is no known record of an inn anywhere in Britain in the 1880s with that specific name. There were, however, many hundreds of post houses in cities and along the main coaching routes of Britain, from the 17th to the 19th Centuries. They were to be found every ten miles or so offering long-distance travellers riding in mail and commercial coaches, some "refreshment" and a bed for the night, if required, and most importantly, a change of post horses and post boys to drive them at speed to the next post or stage on their journey. Hence the phrase "poste haste" (which occurs no less than three times in the Diary) meaning very fast. Liverpool's post houses were situated in Dale Street, the route along which all mail and other coaches entered or left Liverpool, and very close to Maybrick's offices in Tithebarn Street and to the Cotton Exchange. The diarist writing about "the Poste House" in 1888/89 could well have been referring generically to his favourite post house, without naming it, in the same way people today talk about "going to the pub".

Although the coming of the railways in the 1830s led to a rapid decline in the demand for post houses as the century progressed, the buildings usually survived as pubs. The signage of many post houses was still commonly to be seen well into the 20th Century, such as the display of "Posting House" on the frontage of The Angel in Ilford. A photograph of the inn, circa 1905, is shown overleaf. Another coaching inn, The Castle in Woodford Green, Essex, which had been a post house on the London to Norwich road, had prominent signage up to the First World War advertising: "Carriages and Posthorses to Let". It would not therefore have been at all anachronistic for the diarist to have referred to a post house in the 1880s. Indeed, exactly one century later, the phrase became very well-known again, when Charles Forte established a major country-wide chain of "Post House" hotels to appeal to late 20th Century travellers, looking for the traditional values of good food and hospitality.

There is, however, another very likely explanation for the reference to "the Poste House" in the Diary. The writer could well have been referring to the Old Post Office, a tavern built around 1840 on the actual site of the former Liverpool Post Office in Old Post Office Place, off Church Street, prior to its relocation to larger premises in Canning Place. The inn continues to this day to offer fine "refreshment", and is situated just one minute's walk from Church Alley, where James Maybrick was brought up.

In the absence of any credible evidence being produced over the last 20 years or so to prove that the Diary is a recent forgery, my plea to researchers is to turn their attention to investigating how and why the document came to be written around the years of 1888/89, and to search for the identity of its Victorian author. My view, for what it's worth, is that the Diary was written by James Maybrick, but I remain open to the possibility of another contender.

*

Note: Sadly, I was informed in early February 2016 by his sister Elaine that Michael Barrett was found dead at his home in Southport on 29th January 2016.

Original article copyright © Robert Smith 2013
Revised article copyright © Robert Smith 2016

The Maybrick Diary refers to "the Poste House". This photograph, circa 1905, shows The Angel, a popular Posting House in Ilford, where post horses could be hired to take coach travellers to the next post or stage on the London to Ipswich road

2014

THE METROPOLITAN POLICE AND WORKING-CLASS WOMEN IN THE LATE 1880s

DAVID TAYLOR

This article appeared in edition 54 of The Whitechapel Journal

It is well known that the Ripper murders exposed a number of serious shortcomings in the Metropolitan police force, not least the attitudes of many of its members, irrespective of rank, towards those working-class women who had been murdered in 1888. Such attitudes were not confined to the men who policed Whitechapel. Through an examination of two cases – well-known at the time but largely ignored by later historians – it will be argued that there was what a later generation might call 'institutional sexism' that not only hampered the investigation of some particularly gruesome murders but also raised wider questions about the extent to which class and gender assumptions undermined the oft-repeated claim that the distinctiveness of British policing, as epitomised by the Metropolitan police, was to be found in the notion of 'policing by consent'.

Elizabeth Cass does not figure large in the social history of late-Victorian Britain; Annie Coverdale not at all but in the second half of 1887 and throughout most of 1888 their names were to be found in every newspaper of the day and the rights and wrongs of their cases were even discussed in parliament.[1] Of these two women more is known about Elizabeth Cass. A 23-year old dressmaker from Stockton, she came to London in the summer of 1887 to take up a position with Madame Bowman in Southampton Row, Holborn. Some three weeks after she had taken up employment, on the evening of Coronation Day (28th June), she was walking through a crowd outside Jay's London General Mourning Warehouse in Regent Street when she was arrested by P C Endacott. Endacott was known as a zealous officer, reputedly arresting three or four (alleged) prostitutes a week. He claimed to have been watching Cass for some while before arresting her for soliciting. She was taken to Tottenham Court Road police station and would have been detained overnight but for the intervention of her employer, Madame Bowman. Described as 'modest-looking and neatly-dressed', Cass appeared the following day before Mr Newton, an irascible magistrate, at Marlborough-street police court, where she continued her denial of the charge brought against her. Madame Bowman also appeared and gave evidence as to the respectability of her employee. No witnesses were produced to corroborate Endacott's testimony. The case was dismissed but Mr Newton, the magistrate clearly believed Endacott's story that she had been out for 'an improper purpose' and told her that if she were 'an honest girl ... she would not walk in Regent Street at night'.[2] To force home the point, Newton made clear that if Cass appeared in his court again she would face a fine or even imprisonment.

The matter might have ended there but for the determination of Mrs Bowman who wrote to the Home Secretary. The case was raised in the House of Commons on the 7th July 1887 by H J Wilson (MP for the West Riding of Yorkshire) and Llewellyn Atherley Jones (MP for NW Durham). Such was the coverage given to the incident that Wilson received over 400 letters of support after he had spoken in the Commons. The government, refusing to set up an inquiry, was defeated in a vote on 5 July 1887, before performing a volte face on the question the following day. Sir Charles Warren (the Metropolitan police commissioner) held an inquiry to determine whether action should be taken against PC Endacott for perjury. Although the police enquiry concluded that Endacott had made an 'honest mistake', he was sent for trial on a charge of perjury. The trial opened at the Old Bailey in October 1887, and once again Elizabeth Cass's personal history was subjected to close scrutiny. The trial finished sensationally when Justice Stephens instructed the jury to return a verdict of 'not guilty'.[3] Endacott was then reinstated on full pay. Neither decision was well received.

Much less is known about Annie Coverdale beyond the incident in Canning Town which led to her arrest by PC Bloy in January 1888.[4] A 'respectable' domestic servant, she had gone out to buy some milk when she chanced upon her 'young man', who was drunk. Trying to get him back to his lodgings, the two were set upon and the 'young man' had a watch and chain and money stolen. Coverdale held on to one of the attackers while neighbours called the police. PC Bloy, refused Coverdale's plea to arrest the thief, and arrested her for drunk and disorderly behaviour. Bloy gave evidence to the court at West Ham the following day, describing in vivid terms how a drunken Coverdale was fighting in the street with two men, one of whom was 'naked to the skin'. He informed the court that he had known her for two or three years and that for every night in the last three or four months she had been walking out with 'sailors or seafaring men' up to twelve or one in the morning'.[5] Bloy's evidence was supported by a colleague, PC Hatfield.[6] When it transpired that Coverdale had lived in Canning Town for only one year he modified his evidence, claiming to have known her for a year. However, as one reporter noted, Bloy's 'most venomous descriptions ... [were] so recklessly given that its inaccuracies were at once palpable.'[7] The magistrate, Mr Baggallay was unimpressed, stating that he did not believe Bloy's evidence 'at all' and dismissed the case.[8] It subsequently transpired that Coverdale had been kicked and punched by Bloy. Warren held an inquiry into the incident and exonerated Bloy (who was re-instated and moved to a new district, Poplar) and criticized the magistrate for coming 'to so hasty a decision'. Coverdale's case was also raised in parliament but no further action was taken against Bloy, giving rise to further concerns about the attitudes and actions of senior policemen.⁹ Although the two incidents had taken place in very different parts of London, they were quickly linked. For Stead, at the *Pall Mall Gazette*, it was an opportunity to continue his campaign against Commissioner Warren; the Coverdale incident became 'the Cass case of Canning Town' and PC Bloy 'the Endacott of the East End'.[10]

The problems experienced by Cass and Coverdale were not unique.[11] Further, as several contemporary commentators observed, there were fundamental questions to be asked about the right of women to be in the street, without being seen to be prostitutes, and about way in which women were treated by the police (and magistrates) at a time when once-traditional male territory, particularly but not exclusively in the West End, was being occupied – invaded, some would see it – by middle- and working-class women on a scale never experienced before. It was not simply a question of the threat to 'respectable' middle-class women of false arrest or false accusations about their behaviour. Working-class women and those deemed not to be 'respectable' were even more at risk, running a higher probability of falling foul of what many saw as 'growing insolence and criminal boldness of the [police] rank and file' on the streets of London but which never came to public attention.[12] One court missionary, commenting on the 'suffering and misery caused by the over-officiousness and evil imagination of the police' believed that there were 'scores – maybe hundreds – of women and girls who judge it more expedient to suffer in silence'.[13] The radical press, arguing that Endacott and Bloy were symptomatic of a more systemic failure, similarly referred to 'the tyranny exercised on the poor by the London police'.[14]

An already problematic situation was compounded by the speed and manner with which the police authorities sought to protect and then exonerate their much-criticised men. 'The police are moving heaven and earth in the endeavour to screen their fellow-constable Endacott', claimed one leading provincial paper.[15] The police inquiry set up by Warren had been 'conduct[ed] in a manner as though the question at issue was the credibility not of PC Endacott, but of Miss

Cass'.[16] Endacott's reinstatement was seen as a signal from Scotland Yard 'if not quite "Tell a lie and stick to it," then certainly "If you blunder, never own up."'[17] Similarly, the exoneration of Bloy (and the criticism of the magistrate involved in the Coverdale case) confirmed the belief that the police authorities were high-handed and cared more about the protection of fellow-officers than of the public at large. The *Pall Mall Gazette* ran a highly critical article under the headline 'THE WHITEWASHING OF ST. BLOY' while *Reynolds's Newspaper* felt it necessary to reassert the fact that 'the police exist for the people'.[18]

Contemporary responses to these two cases are illuminating. Direct evidence of popular attitudes is extremely difficult to come by but there were clear indications of unease and anger in the letters of support for Elizabeth Cass that flooded into the offices of the *Pall Mall Gazette* and the angry questions asked by certain residents of West Ham as they met to protest outside their local town hall.[19] The radical press was much exercised by the two cases and claimed to speak on behalf of a larger, predominantly working-class constituency in its outspoken condemnations. Policemen, deliberately and persistently lying, and a commissioner, high-handedly and unjustifiably exonerating his men, were roundly condemned in the pages of *Lloyd's Weekly*, *Pall Mall Gazette* and *Reynolds's Newspaper* where ringing denunciations of 'the arrogance of the police' and 'police tyranny' were made.[20] Such criticism went beyond the short-comings of an individual and suggested a systemic fault – an institutionalised bias against working-class women and men. Considerable sympathy, most notably by Stead in the *Pall Mall Gazette*, was expressed for 'Cass-like people' (that is respectable women) but a number of radical papers made more wide-ranging criticisms of 'the high-handed fashion in which custodians of law and order treat the outcasts of the pavement'.[21] There was also the question of hypocrisy and class bias. *The Pall Mall Gazette*, reminding its readers of an earlier scandal in which corruption had been covered up, asked rhetorically:

What are the public to think of a police force under which a

MINIHAN is dismissed for refusing to keep silent about Mrs Jefferies's bribes and an ENDACOTT is reinstated after bringing foul and baseless charges against an innocent girl?[22]

As a consequence of police behaviour in these two cases, it was widely concluded that there was 'a feeling of mutual distrust' as a 'once popular body' had been brought 'into such abject disgrace.'[23]

The police were also subjected to ridicule. Even before his trial had taken place, PC Endacott found himself (and Elizabeth Cass) in a hastily rewritten libretto for the comic opera, *The Sultan of Mocha*, which was running at the Strand Theatre.[24] The satirical magazine Fun published a number of parodies based on Gilbert and Sullivan's 'A policeman's lot ...' while another satirical publication, *Funny Folks* published a number of spoof letters, including one from 'AN ADMIRER OF ENDACOTT' who castigated 'unscrupulous politicians [who] are refusing to acknowledge that the average man becomes a first-class angel directly he puts on the uniform of the constabulary'.[25] Bloy also came in for comment. 'A thing of falsehood is a Bloy for ever' or so *Funny Folks* opined before running the following spoof advertisement.

> METROPOLITAN POLICE – TENDERS FOR WHITEWASH
>
> *The stock of whitewash at Scotland Yard, in consequence of the extraordinary demands made upon it in connection with Endacott, Bloy and the charges of blackmail, having been exhausted. Tenders are now invited for the supply of a quantity sufficient for the coming year. Samples must be submitted to Sir Charles Warren, and must be guaranteed to be of a consistency which will readily cover up the blackest case.*[26]

Criticised, then ridiculed – this was not the Metropolitan police's finest hour. The cartoon on the following page from *Funny Folks* captures the mood perfectly.

The Cass and Coverdale cases confirmed fears that members of the Metropolitan police were high-handed, even criminal, in their treatment of working-class women; dishonest in the way in which they gave (in some cases fabricated) evidence against those they had arrested and also in support of colleagues; and that senior figures

TIME WORKS "WINDERS."

DESIGN FOR A STAINED-GLASS WINDOW TO BE ERECTED IN SCOTLAND YARD. SIR CHARLES WARREN HAVING PENSIONED ENDACOTT, NOW GIVES BLOY THE "WHITE FLOWER OF A BLAMELESS LIFE," AND CROWNS HIM WITH LAUREL FOR HIS HEROIC CONDUCT. IN THE BACKGROUND THE LION (OF TRAFALGAR SQUARE) LIES DOWN WITH THE LAMB.

tolerated (indeed seemed to reward) such behaviour, even in the face of magisterial, parliamentary and press condemnation. That some of this condemnation was an oversimplification, even wrong, is beside the point. There was widespread concern that justice was not being dispensed. Cass and Coverdale were not seen as isolated cases. Both were determined women, and both (to a greater or lesser extent) had support from employer, family and neighbours but they were not alone in being wrongfully accused – many other women as well as men found themselves in that position but most probably accepted their fate as unjust but unavoidable. Endacott and Bloy, likewise, were not seen as untypical 'rotten apples'. Cases of women and men being charged, even found guilty, on the uncorroborated evidence of a policeman are to be found hidden away in the pages of the local press. If Cass and Coverdale gave names and faces to a larger body of wrongly accused women; Endacott and Bloy embodied a wider police culture that impinged not only on suspected prostitutes but drunks, beggars, street hawkers, traders, entertainers and the like. Viewed in this wider context the belated and unsatisfactory response of the Metropolitan police to the Whitechapel murders is unsurprising.

References

1 For a fuller discussion of the issues raised by these cases and the broader context in which they occurred see D Taylor, 'Cass, Coverdale and Consent: The Metropolitan Police and working-class women in late-Victorian London' *Cultural & Social History*, vol.12, 2015, 113-136.

2 The case was widely reported but see *Lloyd's Weekly Newspaper*, 10 July 1887, *Pall Mall Gazette*, 4 July 1887, *Leeds Mercury*, 9 July 1887 and *Reynolds's Newspaper*, 10 July 1887.

3 Details of the trial can be found at www.OldBaileyonline.org (t18871024-1058), accessed 22 August 2013. For the discussions in parliament see *Hansard*, HC Deb 7 July 1887, 22 July, 9 August 1887 and 22 August 1887.

4 For initial press coverage see *Standard*, 26 Jan. 1888 and *Pall Mall Gazette*, 26 January 1888. For the parliamentary discussion see *Hansard*, HC Deb 10 February 1888, 13 February 1888 and 20 March 1888.

5 *North-Eastern Daily Gazette*, 26 January 1888.

6 *Standard*, 26 January 1888. See also *Daily News*, 28 January 1888 and *North-Eastern Daily Gazette*, 28 January 1888.

7 *Ipswich Journal*, 27 January 1888.

8 Coverdale was more fortunate than Rosa Parton whose accusation of violence against PC Butler was dismissed as 'lies' by the magistrate at Bow-street. Parton's allegation was subsequently withdrawn, allegedly because the magistrate was unsympathetic to a case that had been supported by the Society for the Protection of Women and Children. The medical evidence appears to support Parton's claim that she had been the victim of punches rather than 'an accidental push' as Butler claimed. *Hansard*, House of Commons debate 28 July 1887, *The Standard*, 23 July, 1887, *Pall Mall Gazette*, 29 July & 1 August 1887, *Morning Post*, 5 August 1887.

9 *Daily News*, 31 January 1888, *Pall Mall Gazette*, 1 & 2 February 1888, *Reynolds's Newspaper*, 5 & 19 February 1888.

10 *Pall Mall Gazette*, 28 Jan 1888.

11 For example, Sophia Porter was charged with soliciting in November 1866 but the case against her was flawed because of the incomplete, contradictory and uncorroborated police evidence (*Lloyd's Weekly Newspaper* 18 November 1866); similarly, Catherine Clement was arrested for soliciting at London Bridge Railway Termini in May 1869 and the uncorroborated evidence of the arresting policeman rejected by the magistrate (*Reynolds's Newspaper*, 16 May 1869); and the charge of soliciting against Esther Cook in August 1879 was thrown out by Mr Newton (of

Cass notoriety) because of the absence of credible police evidence. Cook made a number of serious allegations about police harassment involving several constables and several women. A police inquiry showed the allegations to be true but no further action was taken as none of the women were prepared to lay charges. (*Reynolds's Newspaper*, 14 August 1870).

12 *Reynolds's Newspaper*, 11 March 1888.
13 *Pall Mall Gazette*, 4 November 1887.
14 *Reynolds's Newspaper*, 10 & 31 July 1887. See also 5 February and 21 March 1888.
15 *Birmingham Daily Post*, 18 July 1887.
16 *Birmingham Daily Post*, 27 July 1887.
17 *Pall Mall Gazette*, 3 November 1887.
18 *Pall Mall Gazette*, 21 March 1888 and *Reynolds's News*, 25 March 1888. Space precludes a more detailed consideration of the issues raised by these cases but see Taylor, 'Cass, Coverdale and consent' for a fuller discussion.
19 *Hansard*, House of Commons debate 21 March 1888.
20 For example *Lloyd's Weekly Newspaper*, 10 July 1887; *Pall Mall Gazette*, 7 July 1887; *Reynolds's Newspaper*, 25 March, 10 July 1888, 15 January 1888 & 25 March 1888. For a fuller discussion of the range of press responses see Taylor, 'Cass, Coverdale and consent'.
21 *Pall Mall Gazette*, 7 July 1887. See also *Englishwoman's Review*, 15 July 1887, which identified prostitutes, drunks and attempted suicides as groups at risk from the police.
22 *Pall Mall Gazette*, 3 November 1887. Inspector Minahan reported an incident of bribery at Mrs Jefferies's high-class brothels but no action was taken. He was laughed at and warned about what he said. Demoted to sergeant he finally resigned from the force. *Pall Mall Gazette*, 11 April 1885, *Lloyd's Weekly Newspaper*, 19 April 1885.
23 *Graphic*, 6 August 1887 and *Reynolds's News*, 12 February 1888.
24 *Lloyd's Weekly Newspaper*, 2 October 1887.
25 *Funny Folks*, 5 November 1887. A regular feature, 'The Wiggery's at Breakfast' commented on the Cass case (see 5 & 12 November 1887) and Warren and his exonerated men were parodied in a sketch, 'Warren the Wunth' (11 February 1888).
26 *Funny Folks*, 18 February 1888. It also noted the paradox 'That Bloy should be a Pop'lar constable'. Even members of parliament joined in. The MP for Cork, Dr. Tanner, referring to the proposal to strike a Jubilee medal for the police, suggested, with heavy-handed humour, that it 'commemorate another proceeding in which the police are concerned, and recall the features of the celebrated Miss Cass'. *Hansard*, House of Commons debate 15 July 1887.

2015
A LETTER TO THE HOME SECRETARY: THE STATE AND THE RIPPER

CLIVE BLOOM

This article appeared in edition 61 of The Whitechapel Journal

The Whitechapel Murders coincided with the consolidation of the Victorian state, a wholly new organ of control consisting of the Home Office, the Colonial Office, Treasury and the Metropolitan Police, as well as local municipal government. It was a situation wholly undreamt of when Victoria came to the throne in 1837, but fifty years later was an established fact that bewildered those who had grown up in an age of individualism.

Indeed, the idea of a 'state', in any real sense, as those organs of public control unattached and barely answerable to either government, parliament or even the monarchy would have been unthinkable in the eighteenth century. It was still anathema to the Georgians of the period 1789 to 1815 with its French republican implications, and was still unthinkable to those who tried with violence to hold back the tentacles of hated laws and non-regulated control and whose actions culminated in the Cato Street Conspiracy of 1820. Slowly the meaning of the 'state' evolved and the role of government changed, and with these changes so too changed the nature of the 'private' person and the sense of one's own personal space. Social control seemed to threaten to extinguish the singularity of the self that was the cornerstone of Victorian sensibility.

There was no state of any modern type before mid- century because there was little industrialisation, no empire that needed centralised regulation and no population explosion which needed control; London was not yet the 'world city'. Even in the mid-nineteenth century the idea of such over-arching control was still broadly opposed by intellectuals and metropolitan factory owners who had developed a strong sense of self-help and individualism (satirised by Dickens' Mr. Gradgrind in *Hard Times*), backed up by the professional military and police which had come slowly to replace agrarian patronage and county influence backed up by Tory mobs and amateur yeomanry. It was the strange merger of the traditional means of control with the new means of power that effectively created the state organs which had emerged by the 1880s.

Yet it was clear that something momentous had changed. Looking back from 1914, the jurist A V Dicey concluded,

> *The current of opinion had for between thirty and forty years been gradually running with more and more force in the direction of collectivism with the natural consequence that by 1900 the doctrine of laissez faire, ..., had more or less lost its hold upon the English[sic] people. The laws affecting elementary education, the Workmen's Compensation Act of 1897, the Agricultural Holdings Acts, the Combination Act of 1875, the whole line of Factory Acts, the Conciliation Act, 1896, and other enactments ..., though some of them might be defended on Benthamite principles, ... looked at as a whole prove that the jealousy of interference by the State which had long prevailed in England had, to state the matter very moderately, lost much of its influence, and that with this willingness to extend the authority of the State the belief in the unlimited benefit to be obtained from freedom of contract had lost a good deal of its power.*[1]

These provisions of governmental interference had, to all intents and purposes, through the intensification of protectionism and the rise of socialism, broken the belief in free trade and free personal actions and greatly enlarged the role of the state in everyday affairs.

As the state emerged from its embryonic beginnings so too did those organs of working-class life that came to represent what was necessary to combat the new powers structures of big government. The emergence of the new unions of the late 1880s marked the high point of communal opposition before the emergence of the Labour Party and from the late 1880s onwards it was precisely through organisation rather than individualism that progress was thought to be made.

It seemed that endless reform was in the air by the late nineteenth century. In 1888, the Liberal MP Sir William Harcourt exclaimed that 'we are all socialists now', a comment somewhat more facetiously echoed by the Prince of Wales in 1895, and although the two actual socialist parties, the Social Democratic Federation and the Socialist League, were tiny, everyone thought of themselves as a socialist, or, at least, 'an unconscious socialist' as Sidney Webb put it, as long as they supported the vague ideals of reform and its implication: collectivism.

Herbert Spencer, apostle of those liberal virtues so necessary to men of his individualist creed, saw in the Liberal Party those actions which were the very destruction of the principles which it stood for in the first place. These were the principles of that Manchester-style capitalism which put self-help, laissez-faire, low taxes, non-conformism and individualism as the greatest social virtues, and which were now being eroded by the dictatorship of 'pathological' collectivism. For Spencer, whose idea of society was that of a living organism, this amounted to a terminal illness.

> *Dictatorial measures, rapidly multiplied, have tended continually to narrow the liberties of individuals; and have done this in a double way. Regulations have been made in yearly growing numbers, restraining the citizen in directions where his actions were previously unchecked, and compelling actions which previously he might perform or not as he liked; and at the same time heavier public burdens, chiefly local, have further restricted his freedom, by lessening that portion of his earnings which he can spend as he pleases, and augmenting the portion taken from him to be spent as public agents please .... Thus, either directly or indirectly, and in most cases both at once, the citizen is at each further stage in*

> *the growth of this compulsory legislation, deprived of some liberty which he previously had.*[2]

Spencer was deeply perplexed. 'How is it', he asked, 'that Liberalism, getting more and more into power, has grown more and more coercive in its legislation?'

Nowhere was the move towards centralisation and consequent bureaucratisation more obvious than in central government departments, especially the Home Office, which turned from a small government office (albeit an important one) with very few officials, who were chosen because of their position in society, into one of the largest government departments, professionalised and bureaucratised in equal measure and served by a very large network of trained expert inspectors with a remit to pry into many aspects of life that were once thought of as private.

In the early 1850s, attitudes began to thaw at the edges as the work of controlling the country began to fray. In 1854, civil service reformers started finally began work on a report into the permanent organisation of the Home Office beginning from the principle that the growth of the country and therefore the Home Office 'could not be carried on without the aid of an efficient body of permanent officers ... possessing sufficient independence, character, ability and experience to be able to advise, assist, and to some extent, influenced, those who are from time to time set over them'.[3]

Testing for this new breed of civil servant began in April 1856. Further internal re-organisation meant that in 1870 there were 33 officials working centrally. This was a small rise, but one that had the Treasury in a spin over costs. It would be the tension between efficiency and costs that would mark many of the Home Office's future tussles with the Treasury. The Colonial Office also went through a continuous period of restructuring between 1868 and 1872. The necessary extra staff that both departments accrued were not so busy as they might have expected and passed their time making bets on passing vehicles, playing corridor cricket, writing books or poems or kicking their heels. It would be another twenty

A Letter to the Home Secretary: The State and the Ripper

Herbert Spencer

to thirty years before staff were fully employed in the domestic, criminal or general divisions of the Home Office. In 1876, when there were still only 36 central staff in Whitehall.

'Rationalisation, examination and competition' really entered the Home Office in the period from 1876 to 1896 and it was to radically change the outlook and actions of its members. L N Guillamard recorded his own reminiscences of working at The Home Office during this period of change in memoirs written in 1937. He recalled 'a ferment was at work owing to the introduction of the democratic system of entry by competitive examination, which paid no heed to family trees and recognized no aristocracy but that of brains'. It was, perhaps evolution rather than a revolution, from which a large expert cadre of professional bureaucrats would emerge, centralised, controlled and organised as an arm of the new idea of 'big' government, but one that rapidly increased in pace after 1896. By the time of the murders the East End was awash with social investigators, philanthropists, moral reformers, evangelical Christians and socialists of every hew. Such were the auxilleries of state reform and collectivism, more prominent still was the bobby on the beat.

The Metropolitan Police were directly responsible to the Home Office. Despite the police being a civilian force, and despite its Special Branch and detective department outgrowths, it was essentially a uniformed, military style organisation designed to maintain communal order and Metropolitan commissioners ran it as such, officers being recruited from the colonial army with colonial ideas about soldiering and 'native' populations.

The organisation was bureaucratic and hierarchic.[4] It had an establishment of 13,000 men which had grown from 7,000 men in 1870. The uniformed police were there for surveillance as much as for actual presence and to create deterrence, clearing a path through 'obstructions... drunks, vagrants, mischievous children, unlawful street traders and bookmakers' and any other illegal practice which seemed unwholesome.[5] *The Times* suggested (14 September 1883) that the British bobby was now a trusted member of the community,' a friend of the people' rather than regarded as an 'enemy'.[6]

Yet in 1887, the police might still be dropped a sovereign, by the likes of Sherlock Holmes and his class (a perk, not a bribe for men who were still being paid the wages of unskilled workers by 1890). To those in the poorer areas that the police patrolled, the police were an affront to the traditional activities of street life, 'blue locusts' who interfered where not needed. To the working-classes they were trusted and despised in equal measure, for their allegiance was conservative and traditional. They owed their loyalty to that class and those superiors who led them, as was demonstrated to socialist intellectuals after the debacle of 'Bloody Sunday', 13 November 1887.

The Metropolitan Police District covered a radius of 15 miles around Charing Cross and was divided into 22 'divisions', one of which patrolled the Thames. Each division was designated by a letter with H division responsible for Whitechapel based in four police stations: Leman Street; Commercial Street; Stepney; Shadwell. The area was flanked by K and J division. One of the irksome issues which needed urgent attention was the relationship of the police service to the Home Office; a final vicious tug of war with the Commissioner Sir Charles Warren in 1886, established the direct control of the department over a force that believed itself an 'independent' arm of domestic imperial policy. The inability of the Met to catch a 'simple' murderer finally led Warren to resign in November 1888.

In May, 1901 Gustav Maeterlinck, the occultist author of *Der Golem*, published a little book on the life cycle of the honey bee. Called *The Life of the Bee*, it went through twenty five editions between its publication and 1935, and reportedly sold over one hundred thousand copies. Why did anyone queue to get a book that was purportedly a work on the nature of an insect?

Maeterlinck's book seemed to contain a secret code: a commentary on the complex nature of bee behaviour and an essay on contemporary life. In studying bees, Maeterlinck seemed to find the perfect metaphor for the 'loneliness' and isolation of the individual when outside or excluded from the masses, but he also found a means to explain the need for a controlling queen and her return at regular intervals to 'breathe [in] the crowd' dwelling in 'the city'; the queen may be the hub of the wheel of society, but the whole was animated by the selfless effort of the 'workers'.

Such a society was, ironically, a microcosm of Spartan republicanism 'where the individual is entirely merged in the republic, and the republic in its turn invariably sacrifices to the abstract and immortal city of the future'. Such sacrifices as are made by all the organs of the community are aimed at racial improvement and are at the 'cost of the liberty, the rights and the happiness of the individual', for 'as a society organizes itself... so does a shrinkage enter the private life of each of its members'. In order to enhance collective strength private life had to be diminished.

The fears and dreams of late Victorian society are here enumerated as the necessary conditions for the future: collectivism based on the effort of the workers; centralisation and the growing complexity of urban life; the subordination of the individual and individual freedom to race survival, all set against an unchangeable social hierarchy with a queen ensconced at the head of the 'republic', immobile, immured, secret, and magical.

Nevertheless, a new type of person started to emerge in the 1880s as a consequence and as a direct response to collectivisation. Such individualism was epitomised by the publication of Robert Louis Stevenson's *The Strange Case of Dr. Jekyll and Mr. Hyde* in 1886. The double in the book hints at the peculiar dual personality and the hidden and perverse depths of conformist man when he experiments in secret. It is hardly surprising that the period witnessed the creation of the ultra-rational Sherlock Holmes or that his creator was a convinced spiritualist from the beginning. Such dualisms may be seen in the political arena between the events of Bloody Sunday and the Greenwich Bomb Outrage of 15 February, 1894 where the rise of extreme socialist and anarchist protest was predicated on the idea that Victorian life was a feeble sham just waiting to be unmasked.

The more centralised the vision of the state, the more the press and intellectuals focussed on the irrational and chaotic: by the late

1880s the fictional detective existed, not to solve crime *per se*, but to solve crime as *existential threat*. Sherlock Holmes has little to do with the nature of real detection and much to do with making things right in a troubled world. Such anxieties surfaced throughout the period and often came to focus on disaster scenarios which personified evil either in arch –villains such as Professor Moriarty, psychotic anarchists such as Edward Douglas Fawcett's *Hartman the Anarchist* of 1892, or death–dealing aliens as feature in H G Well's *War of the Worlds* (1898).[7] Much of this suggests a shadow world of societal and psychological fears reflecting the normality of the actual world, but in which the abnormal and chaotic may suddenly emerge as reality.[8]

The expansion of both the Home Office and the Metropolitan Police alongside the emergence of a truly national press meant that for the first time individual aberration became national crises. Both the Home Office and Metropolitan Police were the focus for letters written by amateur sleuths, crackpots, journalists and anxious citizens. Henrietta Barnett organised a petition which was signed by 4000 people, the attached letter was printed in the papers and received by the Queen, she left it to the Home Secretary to reply. Victoria, in her turn, took sufficient interest to harass the Home Secretary, forcing Lord Salisbury to hold a cabinet meeting on a Saturday, something unheard of, and all to discuss a reward.[9]

The murders seemed to lead to a crime without clues. Robert Anderson reported to the Home Office on 23 October, 1888 that,

> *That a crime of this kind should have been committed without any clue being supplied by the criminal is unusual, but that five successive murders should have been committed without our having the slightest clue of any kind is extraordinary, if not unique in the annals of crime.*[10]

The police seemed left-footed and impotent. Warren had already experimented with using bloodhounds (to the derision of the press) and had got a dressing down from the Home Secretary when he ordered the famous graffiti referring to the 'Juwes' to be removed before a photograph was taken; 80,000 handbills had been circulated, 2,000 lodgers questioned; Greeks, gypsies, circus cowboys and even John Burns the union leader detained. Seventy six butchers and slaughterers and numerous suspects reported to the police by locals were questioned and released and all to no effect.[11] Were the police even looking in the right direction? To the press the police simply appeared bewildered. *The East End News* of 5 October, 1888, commented on the 'marvellous inefficiency of the police' whilst others noted the disregard for protective and preventative patrols in poorer areas of London.[12]

All that was left was the speculation: the murderer was be everyone from an anarchist terrorist, to a twisted social reformer, mad doctor, psychotic aristocrat or homicidal immigrant of Jewish or 'Asiatic' background as Robert Anderson speculated; even the name, Jack the Ripper was speculation. E W Hornung, alongside others, thought that Jack was a 'really eminent public figure', a speculation so potent as to have remained the dominant version of the killer in popular culture; the national loss of confidence in the police finally lead to major reforms in 1894. The police of the 1880s certainly were not the efficient and heroic Scotland Yard detectives that became to staple of literature and film in the 1920s.

The murders represented a type of national neurosis, a rent in the normality of a growingly conformist society. Mary Hughes, a West End school teacher recalled the pervasive and unsettling nature of the crimes, whose miasmic contagion took on gothic proportions.

> *How terrified and unbalanced we all were by the murders. It seemed to be round the corner, although it all happened in the East End, and we were in the West; but even so, I was afraid to go out after dark, if only to post a letter. Just as dusk came on we used to hear down our quiet and ultra-respectable Edith Road the cries of newspaper boys in tones made as alarming as they could: 'Another 'orrible murder ... Whitechapel! Disgustin' details ... Murder!*[13]

Our fascination with Jack the Ripper may be understood as the first breath of a distinct type of individualistic perversity, informing popular culture, communal nostalgia and rebellious concepts of the self. It also explains our own perverse fascination with murder

A Letter to the Home Secretary: The State and the Ripper

and detection: the secret histories of those who do not choose to be known. Jeremy Paxman in his book *The English* comments on the English obsession with privacy, and Jack the Ripper surely is the most private person in history.[14] He (or she) may not have been English born, but the killer certainly appeals to a very 'English' sensibility, in the face of greater and greater aggregation. It is ironic, given the ideology of collectivism and centralisation, that the state was never able to stabilise and control the identity of the person who eluded its control through the autumn of 1888.

References

1 A V Dicey, *Lectures on the Relation between Law & Public Opinion in England During the Nineteenth Century* (London: Macmillan, 1948) xxx -xxxi
2 Herbert Spencer quoted in *Beatrice Webb, My Apprenticeship* (London: Longmans, Green and Co., 1926) 32
3 The information regarding the Home Office is reprinted from chapters 13 and 14 of Clive Bloom, *Victoria's Madmen: Revolution and Alienation* (Basingstoke: Palgrave Macmillan, 2013) reproduced with permission of Palgrave Macmillan.
4 Louise A Jackson 'Law, Order and Violence' in Alex Werner, ed., *Jack the Ripper and the East End* (London: Chatto and Windus, 2008) 100
5 Ibid., 102
6 Jeremy Paxman, *The English* (Harmondsworth: Penguin,1999) 139
7 Edward Douglas Fawcett, *Hartman the Anarchist* (London: Bone, 2009)
8 Individuality as essentially perversity was first explored by Edgar Allan Poe and later by Fyodor Dostoyevsky in *Notes from Underground* (1864)
9 Judith Walkowitz, 'Narratives of Sexual Danger' in Alexandra Warwick and Martin Willis eds., *Jack the Ripper: Media, Culture, History* (Manchester: Manchester University Press, 2007) 188
10 Andrew Smith, 'The Whitechapel Murders and the Medical Gaze' in Warwick and Willis, 116
11 Report of Chief Inspector Swanson to the Home Office 19 October, 1888 in Robert F Haggard, 'Jack the Ripper as the threat of Outcast London' in Warwick and Willis, 205
12 William J Fishman, Crime and Punishment' in Warwick and Willis, 232
13 Walkowitz, 189
14 Paxman, 118

Information on the Home Office first appeared in Chapter 13 of *Victoria's Madmen: Revolution and Alienation* (Palgrave Macmillan: 2013).

www.ingramcontent.com/pod-product-compliance
Lightning Source LLC
Chambersburg PA
CBHW060655100426
42734CB00047B/1825